My name is

I was baptized

on

at

My godparents were…

Text by Lois Rock
Illustrations copyright © 2011 Sophy Williams
This edition copyright © 2016 Lion Hudson IP Limited

The right of Sophy Williams to be identified as the illustrator
of this work has been asserted by her in accordance with the
Copyright, Designs and Patents Act 1988.

Published by
Lion Children's Books
www.lionhudson.com
Part of the SPCK Group
SPCK, 36 Causton Street, London, SW1P 4ST

ISBN 978 0 7459 7661 7

First edition 2016

Acknowledgments

Bible extracts are taken or adapted from the Good News Bible ©
1994 published by the Bible Societies/HarperCollins Publishers Ltd
UK, Good News Bible © American Bible Society 1966, 1971, 1976,
1992. Used with permission.

A catalogue record for this book is available from the British
Library

Printed and bound in China, August 2022, LH54

The Lion
BAPTISM
*B*IBLE

RETOLD BY LOIS ROCK
ILLUSTRATED BY SOPHY WILLIAMS

LION
CHILDREN'S

CONTENTS

THE OLD TESTAMENT

THE NEW TESTAMENT

In the Beginning

Darkness. Utter darkness.

Shapeless, shifting, like the ocean depths.

And God. God's voice, commanding…

"Let there be light!"

At once the light shone, bright and clear.

God divided the light from dark: the first day, the first night.

On the second day God spoke again. "Come, sky. Be a dome of blue amid the water."

Evening came, and morning: the second day.

God spoke again:

"Water, flow into rivers, lakes, and seas. Let the land appear."

To the new, moist earth, God said, "Waken the seeds of life. Let there be leaves and trees and every kind of plant."

As a third evening faded, the earth was clothed in green.

On the fourth day, God set a golden sun in the sky. As the blue faded to grey, a silver moon appeared, and twinkling stars.

Evening had come to the fourth day, and morning came to the fifth.

"Let there be fish in the sea," said God. "Let birds fly in the sky."

And so it was, and birdsong greeted the sixth day's dawn. "Let there be animals of every kind," said God.

"Let them run on the plains, and prowl the forests. Let them graze the pastures and drink from clear pools.

"And now, let there be human beings. Let them be a true reflection of their Maker. Let them take care of this good world."

The sun set. The seventh day dawned. "From now until the end of time," said God, "let the seventh day be a day of rest for all creation."

PARADISE LOST

The first man, God named Adam. The first woman, God named Eve.

Their home was a paradise garden in Eden.

"Everything here is for you to enjoy," God said. "The trees are heavy with fruit that is yours to pick.

"Only the tree in the middle of the garden is forbidden. If you eat its fruit, you will have to choose between good and evil to the day you die."

For a while all was well. Then one day a snake came and whispered to Eve, "Why has God forbidden you to eat that delicious fruit?"

"It will harm us," replied Eve. "We will no longer be at home in paradise. We will live in a world where good and evil are intertwined. In the end, we will die."

Sss, sss, sss. The snake snickered and hissed.

"Sly, lying God! The truth is, you will become wise. As wise as God.

"Go on. Find out for yourself. Try some fruit."

Eve was tempted. She reached out and picked some.

She bit into a fruit.

"Mmm. It's delicious," she said. Then she called out, "Adam! Come and try this fruit."

Adam came and saw what Eve had done. He too was tempted. He ate the fruit too. He agreed that it tasted wonderful.

Then, in a flicker of light, everything changed. Adam and Eve saw the world differently.

For the first time, they noticed they were naked. For the first time, they felt embarrassed and ashamed.

They made clothes from leaves to hide their nakedness.

In the evening, God came to walk with them and talk with them.

Adam and Eve tried to hide, but God found them.

"Why did you disobey me?" asked God. "Now you will have to leave the paradise garden. No more will we walk and talk as friends.

"You must go out into the wide world. You will toil for a living among its thorns and thistles."

God made clothes of animal skins for his people before he sent them from paradise. Angels stood and guarded the gate. Adam and Eve wept.

Was there no way back to God?

THE GREAT FLOOD

The people God made had children, grandchildren, and great-grandchildren.

The more they grew in number, the more they grew wicked. The time came when God looked in dismay at the quarrels and the fighting. There was only one good man: Noah.

God spoke to Noah: "I am going to send a flood," he explained. "It will end this world's wickedness.

"You are to build a boat: an ark. It must be big enough for you and your family, and also for a pair of every kind of animal, and yet more of your flocks."

Noah did as God said. When he and his family and all the animals were safe on board, God sent a torrent of rain: the water poured down day after day after day.

The world disappeared beneath the flood. The ark floated higher than the mountains. Weeks passed, and months.

These were desolate times, dull and terrifying together. A grey sky. Dark waters.

One day, terror struck everyone on board. The ark lurched violently, and they heard the sound of its timbers crunching and cracking.

The vessel had grounded on a mountaintop.

Slowly, slowly, the flood trickled away.

Noah let a raven fly free to explore, but it simply flew away.

A week later, Noah sent out a dove. It returned with a fresh green twig from an olive tree.

Soon the ground around the ark was dry too. "It is time to leave the ark," said God to Noah. "The animals will be able to make homes and have young.

"Your sons and their wives will have children and grandchildren.

"And look: there is my rainbow in the sky. It is the sign of my promise never to flood the world like this again. There will be summer and winter, seedtime and harvest for ever."

God's Promise to Abraham

Long ago, in the city of Ur, lived a man named Abram.

His wife, Sarai, listened in astonishment to the news he brought.

"My father Terah has plans for the family. We are going to go to Canaan, far to the west. We will make a future for ourselves there."

Sarai smiled hopefully. Maybe everything would go well in Canaan. Maybe she would have children. Maybe she would be the mother of a growing family with a bright future.

Everyone was in good spirits as they set out. However, when they reached the city of Haran, Terah changed his mind.

"This is a good place," he explained to his family. "We can make a new home for ourselves here."

Abram was loyal to his father. However, when Terah grew old and died, Abram still yearned to go to Canaan.

"I hear God telling me to go there," he explained to Sarai. "I hear God promising to bless our family. We will have children and grandchildren. We will be a great nation.

"We will bring God's blessing to all the nations of the world."

It was not long before they set out: Abram and Sarai, Abram's nephew Lot, all the household slaves, and all the family's flocks.

They lived as nomads in the land of Canaan. If they found pasture, they would set up camp and graze the animals.

When there was no grazing left, they would move on.

The sheep and goats and cattle prospered and their numbers grew. The time came when Abram and Lot agreed to go separate ways to make their own living.

But although Abram was wealthy, he and Sarai still shared a great sorrow: they had no children.

"What use is my wealth if I have no son to inherit it?" he complained aloud one night.

Once again, God spoke to him.

"Look up at the stars in the sky," said God. "One day your children will be as many as that."

ABRAHAM, SARAH... AND ISAAC

The years went by. Sarai herself despaired of having
children. Surely she was now too old?

God spoke again:

"Abram: I keep my promises.

"I am giving you a new name – Abraham, and
the word means 'father of many nations'.

"Sarai will have a new name too: Sarah, and the
word means 'princess'.

"The promise I make to you is also a promise to your family for ever: it is an everlasting covenant.

"I will be your God. Your descendants will be my people.

"The land of Canaan will be their home."

Then, after so many years of sorrow, Sarah became pregnant.

She gave birth to a son.

They named him "Isaac", and the name means "laughter".

THE STORY OF ISAAC

Isaac was Abraham's pride and joy.

He had a son! A son who would inherit his wealth! A son who would have children and grandchildren!

Then God spoke again.

"Abraham, I want you to take your son to a mountaintop.

"There, I want you to sacrifice him to me."

It was an astonishing request. Wasn't Abraham dismayed beyond measure?

It was part of Abraham's traditions to offer animals as sacrifice… but a child? No, surely…

Even so, Abraham did as God asked. He set out for a mountaintop. He took with him live coals. He asked Isaac to carry the firewood. When they reached the place, he built an altar of stone.

Then Abraham seized Isaac, tied him up, and laid him on the altar. He raised a knife… and God spoke.

"Abraham… stop.

"You were willing to obey me, though you love Isaac deeply."

Abraham looked around. He saw a ram with its horns caught in a thorn bush.

"Now I understand," he sighed. "God has provided this ram for the sacrifice instead."

God spoke again:

"I will bless you because of your obedience. I will give you many descendants.

"Other nations will ask me to bless them as I have blessed you."

So Isaac grew to be a man. Abraham arranged his marriage to a young woman from among his faraway relatives.

Her name was Rebecca. Isaac fell in love with her the moment he saw her.

In time they had twin sons: Esau and Jacob.

JACOB AND ESAU

Isaac was proud of his firstborn son.

From the time he was a baby he seemed strong and daring. When he grew up, he proved himself to be a skilful hunter.

"I am glad that Esau will get the firstborn's share of my inheritance," Jacob used to say to himself. "I will die content."

Rebecca preferred the younger twin: Jacob. He liked to stay at home and busy himself with household tasks.

One day, Jacob was cooking some bean soup. Esau came home from hunting.

"I'm starving," he declared. "I need some soup."

Jacob turned slowly to look at him.

"I'll want something in return," he said.

He paused. Esau glared impatiently.

"I want your rights as the firstborn," said Jacob.

"Done!" snorted Esau. "I'll die if I don't eat."

Time passed, and Isaac grew older and frailer. His eyesight failed him.

One day he called for Esau. "I want you to go hunting," he said, "and to make a delicious stew with the meat. Then I will give you my final blessing."

Rebecca watched as Esau set out.

"Hurry," she whispered to Jacob. "Go and fetch two goats from the flock. I'll make a stew that you can take to your father. Then he will bless you instead."

Jacob shook his head. "He'll know it's me," he replied. "Esau's skin is rough and hairy. Mine is smooth."

"Don't worry," replied Rebecca. "We can wrap goatskin around your arms to trick the old man. You can wear some of Esau's clothes too."

The plan worked. Isaac enjoyed a bowl of stew, and then he asked God to bless the dear son he was holding in his arms.

Esau returned not long after. He too made a stew and took it to his father.

"But I've just eaten a stew," said Isaac, looking puzzled. "And I've said the blessing."

Esau guessed at once what had happened. He flew into a rage.

Rebecca heard, and she and hurried to Jacob.

"Go – and quickly! Go to my brother Laban, in my childhood home. Hide from Esau until his anger has cooled."

Jacob fled. When night fell, he simply curled up on the ground to sleep. In a dream he saw a stairway to heaven, and angels going up and down along it.

He heard God speaking:

"I am the God of Abraham and Isaac. I will always be with you and I will bless you. I will keep you safe and bring you back to this land, to be your home."

The following day, Jacob journeyed on.

His uncle Laban welcomed him.

"Of course you can come and work for me," he said. "But I must pay you. What can I offer?"

Jacob had already seen Laban's younger daughter: Rachel. He had fallen in love with her.

"I'll give you seven years' work if you let me marry Rachel," he said.

"An excellent agreement!" said Laban.

Seven years flew by and a wedding was arranged.

After the ceremony, Jacob lifted his bride's veil… and drew back in dismay. It wasn't Rachel.

He stormed off to find Laban. "You've tricked me into marrying Rachel's sister, Leah!" he cried.

"It's the custom, dear boy," replied Laban. "First you marry the older sister; then you marry Rachel. Of course, you'll have to work for another seven years…"

Jacob had no choice. He was happy to be married to Rachel, but he could not forgive Laban. He took good care of Laban's flocks, but he took care to build up his own alongside them.

In the end, bitter from years of strife, the two agreed to part.

Jacob and his household set off for the land of Canaan.

All the way he fretted: would he be safe from Esau? What gifts could he offer to mend their quarrel?

Jacob need not have worried. When Esau heard he was coming, he came to meet him – and ran up and hugged him.

"It's good to see you," said Esau. "Let us be glad that we have both prospered; let us forget the old quarrel."

Then he returned to his own home, leaving Jacob to set up a new home in the land of Canaan.

JOSEPH

Jacob's household grew in number. In all, he had twelve sons.

Of these, only the youngest two were the sons of Rachel. Jacob loved Rachel more than the other women in his household, and he loved Joseph and Benjamin more than the other sons.

One day he gave Joseph an elaborately woven cloak. Joseph swaggered around to show it off, and his elder brothers glared in anger.

"It's not just a fine coat," they muttered among themselves. "It's a sign that our father is declaring Joseph his chosen heir."

Joseph believed the same, and it made him proud.

"I had a dream," he told his brothers. "In it, we were gathering the harvest. Your sheaves came and bowed down to mine.

"What do you think that means?"

"It means you're arrogant," replied one.

"We wouldn't bow down to you if our lives depended on it," said another, and they all laughed, menacingly.

Joseph was unstoppable. "And there was another dream," he said one day. "In it, the sun, the moon, and eleven stars bowed down to me."

Even Jacob was alarmed at this.

Had he gone too far in giving privileges to Joseph? Did the young man really think he would rule the family?

One day, Joseph's elder brothers were out in a distant pasture looking after the family flocks.

Jacob sent Joseph to check on what they were doing.

"Here comes the boaster," they grumbled. "Why don't we just get rid of him?"

The eldest, Reuben, suddenly felt uneasy.

"No! That would be wrong. Let's just teach Joseph a lesson. Throw him down the old dry well until he learns to be humble."

So that became the plan. Reuben went about his day's work.

While he was away, the nine remaining brothers saw a caravan of traders passing by.

They sold Joseph as a slave.

Reuben was dismayed to find out what they had done, but he joined with them to cover up the crime. Together they ripped up Joseph's coat and dipped it in animal blood.

When they returned home, they told Jacob that Joseph had been killed by wild animals.

Even in faraway Egypt, God was looking after Joseph. He was bought as a slave by a wealthy man named Potiphar. His honest, hard work gained his master's respect.

Potiphar's wife, however, secretly wanted the young man for herself. When Joseph rejected her advances, she was furious. She told lies about Joseph and had him thrown into prison.

Once again, Joseph proved honest. The jailer trusted him to help with running the prison.

The prisoners liked him too – "Because his God has given him the wisdom to explain dreams," they said.

Among the prisoners were two servants of the Egyptian king, the pharaoh. One night each had a dream. Joseph explained the meaning.

For the baker, it was the worst news: he was to be executed for his wrongdoing.

For the butler, it was the best news: he was to be pardoned.

Both predictions came true, and the butler went back to serving wine in the royal court.

Then the pharaoh himself had two dreams. They bothered him, and he asked his advisors to explain the meaning.

None could do so.

Suddenly the butler remembered Joseph.

"I know someone who can explain even the most puzzling dream," he declared.

The pharaoh sent for Joseph, and Joseph listened.

"In the first dream," said the pharaoh, "I was on the banks of the River Nile. Seven fat cows climbed out of the water on to the bank and began grazing. Then seven thin cows came and ate them.

"After that, I saw seven ears of grain, all plump and full. Then seven more stalks grew. They were thin and dry, and they ate the full ears."

Joseph smiled gravely.

"The two dreams mean the same thing," he said. "There will be seven years of good harvests, and then seven years of famine.

"You need to put someone in charge of storing the harvests from the good years to last during the lean years."

The pharaoh nodded. "I choose you," he said.

So it was that Joseph grew to be wealthy and powerful in Egypt.

He was in charge of selling grain from Egypt's stores when the famine came.

One day, ten brothers arrived from Canaan to buy grain. They bowed lowed to Joseph – not knowing that it was he – as if their lives depended on it.

Joseph recognized them at once. But how could he forgive them? And where was Benjamin?

He questioned them closely, and made a plan. "You say there is another brother? Bring him to Egypt to prove your story!"

Then he sent them away, with sacks full of grain.

The brothers told their father, Jacob, what had happened, but the news nearly broke him. "I lost Joseph long ago," he said. "I can't lose Benjamin as well."

But the famine dragged on, and soon the family had no choice but to make another trip, and take Benjamin to Egypt.

Joseph was delighted to see his younger brother. He welcomed all the brothers and let them have more grain.

However, he told a servant to slip a goblet into Benjamin's sack, without anyone seeing.

When the brothers left, he sent a servant to accuse them of theft and bring them back.

One by one the sacks were searched. The goblet was found in Benjamin's.

"The thief will stay and be punished," thundered Joseph.

Reuben stepped forward.

"Our father will die if you keep Benjamin," he said. "He is still mourning another son, Joseph, who died long ago. Keep me instead."

In that moment Joseph knew his brothers were sorry for what they had done.

"Look again!" he cried. "I am your brother Joseph. I am alive and well. What happened long ago was part of God's plan. Now I can keep you all safe."

He welcomed the entire family to Egypt.

THE STORY OF MOSES

Miriam peered out from among the reeds. The basket her mother had prepared was bobbing gently by the bank in the River Nile.

Inside it was her baby brother. If the pharaoh's soldiers had found him, they would have thrown in him the river to drown.

Those were the orders: the pharaoh who ruled Egypt knew nothing of Joseph, and the story of the family of Jacob. He had made their descendants his slaves, and he treated them cruelly.

Suddenly Miriam heard chattering... and laughter.

She held her breath. One of the royal princesses came down to the water's edge. She had servants with her. She began getting ready to bathe.

She saw something move, and peered among the reeds. "There's something in there," she said to her servant. "Fetch it for me please."

The servant brought the basket. The princess laughed aloud. "It's a baby!" she said. "I think I know why it's there. Someone is trying to save their baby from the soldiers.

"Well: I'm going to keep this little one. I'm going to name him, 'Moses'.

"Now all I need is someone to mother him for me."

Miriam stepped forward. "I know someone who could look after a baby," she said.

"Please bring her!" said the princess.

Miriam fetched her mother. In this way, baby Moses was kept safe.

MOSES AND THE PHARAOH

Moses grew up in luxury as a prince of Egypt.

He knew, however, that he had been born to the descendants of Jacob: the slave people.

One day he went out to the place where the slaves were working; they were mixing mud and straw to make bricks for the pharaoh's fine buildings.

A slave driver had become violently angry with one of them. Moses watched in horror as the slave was beaten to death.

Moses became angry. He hit the slave driver to punish him. The man fell down dead.

Moses was frightened. Hastily he buried the body.

But people had seen him. When Moses knew they might tell, he fled to the wild country. There he met a shepherding family. He married the daughter and looked after his father-in-law's flocks.

One day, when he was out in the pasture, he saw a bush shimmering in the heat. More than shimmering: it was on fire, and yet not burning up.

He walked closer. "Take off your shoes," said a voice. "This is holy ground."

Moses obeyed, trembling. "I am the God of Abraham, Isaac, and Jacob," said the voice. "I have seen how the pharaoh mistreats my people.

"I have chosen you to go and set them free."

Moses was both amazed and dismayed.

"I can't do that!" he argued. "The pharaoh won't listen to me. Anyway, I fall over my words when I speak."

"You can ask your brother Aaron to do the talking," said God. "I will give you the power to work wonders. That will make the pharaoh take notice."

Aaron and Moses went and pleaded with the pharaoh. It was no use: he would not let his slaves go free.

"The slaves will pay for your lack of respect," he told Moses. "Now they will have to collect their own straw to mix with the mud... and still make as many bricks as before."

The people complained bitterly to Moses for making things worse. He went back to the pharaoh. Perhaps a display of God's power would convince him.

Aaron worked a miracle: he showed he could turn his stick into a snake and back again.

Astonishingly the court magicians did the same.

"Such a simple trick," they laughed.

"Pay heed to my warning," declared Moses. "God has real power. God will send disasters to the land of Egypt."

And so it was. The River Nile turned blood red. There was a plague of frogs, and then clouds of gnats and swarms of flies.

The farm animals were struck with a deadly disease. The people got terrible boils from a mystery skin ailment. Hailstorms flattened the crops, and locusts came and consumed any plants that remained. Then the sky went strangely dark.

Still the pharaoh would not let the descendants of Jacob go free.

"I will send one more disaster," God told Moses. "Then the pharaoh will change his mind.

"Tell the people to prepare a special meal with freshly killed lamb. They must mark their doors with its blood.

"Tell them to serve the meal with flatbread made quickly, without yeast.

"They must be ready to make their escape."

Moses gave the message and the people obeyed. The angel of death passed over the houses marked with blood.

In the homes of the Egyptians, which were not marked, the firstborn child and the firstborn of all the animals died.

At last the pharaoh saw that the God of Moses was too strong for him.

"Go!" he told Moses. "Take your people and go."

So they went. For ever after, the descendants of Jacob – the people of Israel – would remember it as Passover: the night when the angel of death passed over them, because God was with them.

THE GREAT ESCAPE

Moses had told the people to be ready for a journey. Even so, it was a rush to get everyone assembled. The nation numbered many thousands. They brought with them flocks of sheep, goats, and cattle.

There was not even enough time to cook the simple bread dough they had prepared, and they brought it along raw. They would bake it only when they felt safe enough to stop and make fire.

Moses walked at the front of the throng. Even so, it was God who led the way. During the day God appeared as a pillar of cloud ahead of them; at night, God's presence was marked by a pillar of fire.

They did not choose the shortest route to Canaan,

but headed south through the wild country before turning again toward the Red Sea.

As the days went by, the pharaoh had time to reflect. What a mistake it had been, he realized, to let his slaves go free!

He gathered his army together and led the pursuit in his own war chariot.

The wheels of 600 chariots churned up a cloud of dust. They rumbled in the ruts and clattered against stones.

The people of Israel turned to look, and were horrified.

"You're to blame for all this!" they screamed at Moses. "We're going to die out here! We were better off as slaves!"

"Don't be afraid," said Moses. "Watch, and see what God will do."

He turned to face the sea and raised his hand.

At once there came a breath of wind that swiftly became a strong breeze.

All night it blew, driving the sea into peaks and troughs. By morning, it had blown the waters into two, leaving a clear path between.

The people of Israel walked along this path to safety.

When the Egyptian army came racing along behind, the sea flowed back over them, and drowned them.

Moses led the people in a victory song:

The Lord is my strong defender;
he is the one who has saved me.
He is my God, and I will praise him,
my father's God, and I will sing
about his greatness.

The people of Israel were safe from the pharaoh, but they had much to learn before God allowed them to enter the land of Canaan.

The hardships they faced taught them to trust in God.

It was God who helped Moses find enough drinking water in the dry and dusty wilderness.

It was God who caused manna to appear like dew on the ground. Every morning the dew dried into sweet flakes, as delicate as frost. They people gathered it to eat.

It was God who sent quails, flying in great flocks into the camp. The people picked them up like chickens and prepared them for the pot.

God spoke again to Moses: "If these people are to be my people, they must do more than enjoy the good things I give. They must also obey me."

GOD'S LAWS

One day, God told Moses to go to the top of a high mountain: Sinai. There, amid thunder and flashes of lightning, God gave Moses ten great commandments:

"I am the Lord your God, who brought you out of Egypt. Worship no gods but me.

"Do not make images of wood and stone, nor treat any such thing as a god.

"Do not claim you are doing what I want when in fact you are doing what you want. That is to take my name in vain.

"Keep the sabbath day of rest.

"Respect your father and your mother.

"Do not murder.

"Do not be unfaithful in marriage.

"Do not steal.

"Do not tell lies accusing people of things they have not done.

"Do not look longingly at the things other people have, but be content with what you have.

"These laws are the heart of an agreement I am making with the people," said God, "an everlasting covenant.

"If the people obey my laws, then I will be their God. They will be my people, I will bring them safely to the land of Canaan and bless them."

The laws were written on two tablets of stone. God gave instructions for making a golden box in which to keep them – the ark of the covenant.

"I want the people to build a place of worship," said God to Moses. "It will be a tent, a tabernacle, that you can take with you when you travel to Canaan.

"Whenever the people look at it, they will know that I am with them. They will remember my laws, and to obey them."

INTO CANAAN

The people spent forty long years wandering the wild country that lay between Egypt and Canaan.

They believed that Canaan was their true home, but they could not simply claim it.

Other peoples lived there and prospered. They would not welcome a band of ragged foreigners!

One day, Moses sent a band of young men to spy out the land and its inhabitants.

They returned with baskets of fruit, and a bunch of grapes so huge it had to be carried on a pole between two people.

"It is a wonderful land," the young men reported, "but it is well defended. The people have built cities with high walls and strong gates."

The news left many discouraged.

"We truly believe that we can make it our own!" argued two of the spies. Their names were Caleb and Joshua. "Come on – God will help us."

They spoke confidently, but they did not change people's minds.

God spoke sternly to Moses. "The people do not trust me. They will suffer the consequences. It will be many years before the nation dares enter the land of Canaan.

"Even you will only glimpse it from afar."

And so the years wore on: weary years of wandering, a nation without a home.

Before Moses died, God chose a new leader to succeed him.

Moses gathered the people together.

"Joshua will be your leader now," he said. "God will lead him to victory over the peoples of Canaan. Be determined and confident. God will never fail you nor abandon you."

THE LAND OF ISRAEL

Joshua stood on the banks of the Jordan. Beyond lay
the land of Canaan: the land he believed God had
promised to the people of Israel.

God's words ran through his mind:

"Just be determined, be confident; and make sure
that you obey the whole Law that my servant Moses
gave you. Do not neglect any part of it and you will
succeed wherever you go."

He needed this reassurance. There would be
many battles to fight.

The first task was for the people of Israel to cross the river.

"Listen," cried Joshua to all the people. "God has told me what to do. The priests must carry the ark of the covenant into the river. When they do, the water will slow to a trickle.

It seemed unlikely. It was the time of year when the river was at its highest.

But Joshua was the leader: the priests obeyed his order to wade in.

To their astonishment, the river did stop flowing.

The people simply walked across.

Joshua led the people into Canaan.

They set up camp outside the city of Jericho.

The first battle would be fought here: against an ancient city with high walls and strong gates. Well-armed Canaanite soldiers looked down menacingly from the battlements.

The Israelites were by contrast bedraggled: travel-weary and under-equipped. But God had a plan. Joshua was bold enough to put it into action.

"God wants the priests to form a procession around the outside of the walls. Some will carry the ark of the covenant. Others will blow trumpets. An armed guard of soldiers will lead and a rear guard will follow behind, in total silence."

The Canaanites watched uneasily from the city walls. The same thing happened on the next day, and the next, for six days.

On the seventh day the procession set off again. This time the people marched around seven times. Then Joshua cried aloud:

"God has given us the city!"

The priests blew their trumpets. The people gave a tremendous shout.

The walls of Jericho collapsed. The people of Israel marched forward and took the city.

That first success gave everyone more hope. Joshua led his fighting force to yet more victories. Little by little they claimed the land of Canaan.

Joshua assigned a portion of land to each of the great families of Israel.

The tent of worship – the tabernacle – was set up in Shiloh.

It was a sign that God and God's people had truly made Canaan their home.

When he was very old, Joshua called the leaders of the people to a great assembly.

"God has kept his part of the covenant. God has given us the land.

"Our part of the covenant is to obey God's laws.

"My household and I promise to do just that.

"What will you choose to do?"

The answer was roared back: "We will serve our God, the Lord."

WARRIORS FOR GOD

Joshua had urged the people to be faithful to their God. For as long as he was alive, they were.

However, they could not help noticing that the tribes of Canaan had different beliefs. They made offerings to the god Baal and the goddess Astarte, and prayed to them for good weather and abundant crops.

All too soon, the people of Israel began to worship at the same shrines, in front of the same idols.

God allowed them to face the consequences of their unfaithfulness.

He let enemy tribes attack them and overpower them.

In the despair of defeat they cried out to God.

"Help us! Have pity on your people!"

From among them God chose warriors who led them to victory.

But as soon as they felt safe, the people forgot their promises to the God of their nation. Once again they gave tribute to the gods of Canaan.

Again they fell prey to their enemies.

Again they repented of their faithlessness.

Again God provided a warrior to defend them.

Again and again and again.

Gideon was an unlikely hero. He was as angry as anyone when the Midianites came raiding. But how could he stop them plundering the harvest crops, or driving away the precious flocks?

One year, he was left with only the remnants of the harvest. He decided to thresh it secretly, inside a wine press.

An angel came and spoke to him: "God has chosen you, brave and mighty man. You are to rescue your people.

"You must begin by tearing down the altar to Baal, and the shrine of Asherah."

Gideon was astonished, but he acted boldly and decisively. His neighbours, at first dismayed, quickly came to respect the young hero.

When he summoned an army, thousands came from far and wide.

"I don't want you to fight with a huge army," God told him. "First send away those who would rather go home.

"Then take those who remain down to the stream to drink. Send away those who kneel down by the water. Keep only those who stay alert as they scoop up water in their hands."

That left Gideon with just 300.

He gave each of them a trumpet, a pottery jar, and a torch that would burn fierce and bright.

"When it is dark," he explained, "we will split into three groups. We will encircle the Midianite camp. The flames must be kept hidden in the jars.

"When my group blows their trumpets, you blow yours. Then smash the jars, hold up the torches, and shout: 'For God and for Gideon.'"

Patiently they waited for the dead of night. When it was time for action…

Rampah pah paaah!

The blaring trumpets and the ring of flame threw the Midianites into confusion. They fought each other before fleeing homewards.

Gideon and his fighters chased them away, and won the victory.

SAMSON

As the years went by, the Philistines became the nation's main enemy. It was at this time that Samson was born. His parents made a promise that he would give his life to serving God. The sign of the promise was to leave his hair uncut.

Samson grew up brave and immensely strong, but he did not act in a godly way. Nor did he shun the Philistines: he even decided to marry a Philistine girl.

On the way to arrange the wedding, he heard a lion roaring. He went and killed it.

On the day of the wedding itself, he went to look at the carcass. He found a swarm of bees inside, and sweet honeycomb.

That gave him an idea: he would set a riddle for the wedding guests.

"Guess the answer," he announced at the wedding party. "There's a prize if you can."

"Out of the eater, something to eat. Out of the strong, something sweet."

The young Philistine men frowned. That really was a puzzle. But they had an idea: ask the bride.

The young woman was more loyal to her people than to her husband. She found out the answer, told the men… and they claimed the prize.

Samson was furious. He began a one-man war against the Philistines. He killed many single-handedly. He set their harvest fields ablaze.

For twenty years Samson harassed the Philistines in this way.

Then he fell in love with another Philistine girl: the dark and lovely Delilah.

She too was faithless, and made a secret plan with the leaders of her own people. She wheedled from Samson the secret of his strength: his long hair, the sign h dedicated to God.

While he was sleeping, she had the long locks cut. The Philistines blinded Samson and dragged him off to prison.

One day, the Philistines were having a riotous celebration.

"Let's get Samson!" they laughed gleefully. "It will be fun to mock the defeated hero!"

The prisoner was put on show between the central pillars of the Philistine temple.

Samson bowed his head. His hair was growing, and it swung across his face. He remembered God, and said a prayer.

Then he put a hand on each of the pillars and pushed.

They cracked and broke. The roof fell in.

With his death, Samson won a mighty victory.

RUTH

For the people of Israel, life was often hard.

Although land of Canaan was rich and fertile, years of bad weather could spoil the crops.

It was during one long famine that Naomi left Bethlehem with her husband and young sons. Together they made themselves a new home. The sons grew up and married local girls.

Then Naomi's husband died, and so did her sons.

"You girls stay here in Moab, and marry again," said Naomi. "I will go to my old home in Bethlehem." They both burst into tears. One of the girls agreed to stay, but the other refused.

"Please let me come with you," pleaded Ruth. "I want to go where you go. Your God will be my God."

Together they made their way to Bethlehem.

It was harvest time.

"We have nothing," said Naomi sadly. "You will have to go gleaning, picking up the leftovers from the harvest fields."

Ruth did so, and she worked hard.

The man who owned the fields was Boaz. He saw how faithful she was being to Naomi. And he fell in love with her.

As soon as he was sure that Ruth loved him in return, he asked to marry her.

Everyone in Bethlehem was delighted when they heard the news of a wedding.

When, in time, Ruth and Boaz had a son, Naomi was the happiest of all.

SAMUEL

Hannah smiled as she brought her little boy to the priest.

"Do you remember me?" she said. "I was at the festival just a few years ago, and you saw me crying and praying.

"You asked God to answer my prayer – whatever it might be.

"Well, here is the answer to prayer: a child of my own. His name is Samuel.

"I promised I would bring him here, to be a helper at the tabernacle."

The priest, Eli, welcomed the little boy and took care of him. Hannah came to visit every year.

As Samuel grew older, Eli taught him the tasks that needed to be done to keep the tabernacle in good order, as was right for a place of worship.

One of the tasks was to sleep in the main part of the tabernacle, ready to refill the lamps on the lampstand when it was needed.

One night, when Samuel was sleeping, he heard a voice.

It called his name. "Samuel! Samuel."

"That must be Eli," said Samuel to himself. He hurried to where Eli was sleeping.

"What do you want me for?" he asked.

"I don't understand! I didn't call you," replied Eli. "Go back to bed and sleep some more."

Samuel obeyed, and soon dozed off.

Then he heard the voice again.

"It MUST be Eli," said Samuel. He hurried to the old man's bedside, and asked again.

"What do you want me to do?"

"You're as mistaken as you were the first time," replied Eli. He sounded a little angry.

"Go back to bed, boy, and stay there."

But the voice came a third time, and a third time Samuel went to Eli.

Then the priest understood.

"It must be God who is calling you," he said. "If the voice calls again, say 'Speak, Lord. Your servant is listening.'"

The voice called again, and Samuel replied as he had been instructed.

It was a harsh message. God told Samuel that Eli's grown-up sons had done all kinds of wicked things. "They are not worthy to be priests," he said. "They are going to face the consequences of their wrongdoing."

Samuel was distressed to hear this. Even so,

when Eli asked what God had said, he had to tell the truth.

Eli sighed at what Samuel told him. He himself was disappointed with his sons.

"God is God," sighed Eli. "He will do what seems best."

At this time, the people of Israel were at war with the Philistines. They asked Eli's sons to carry the ark of the covenant into battle.

It was a disastrous move. The battle was lost, and Eli's sons were killed in the fighting. When Eli heard the news, he was so shocked he died.

Samuel knew his time had come to lead the people in their faith and worship.

"Get rid of all the idols you worship," he said. "The Baals and the Astartes.

"From now on, you must worship our God, and only our God."

A Kingdom, a City, and a Temple

Samuel was judge and prophet in Israel for many years.

He hoped that his sons would follow in his footsteps, but that was not to be. They cared more about money than justice.

The leaders of the people went to Samuel. "You are getting old," they said. "We want you to choose a king to rule us: a king to defend us against the kings of other nations."

Samuel was crushed with disappointment.

"Don't be disheartened," God told him. "The people aren't rejecting you. They are rejecting me.

"First warn them what it is like to have a king: about the way kings demand taxes; about the way they have to give hours of hard labour to keep him in luxury.

"Then, if they insist, choose a king. I will show you who to choose."

The people did insist on a king.

Samuel began to wonder how he would find the right person. "I will send you the young man I want," God told him. "He comes from the least powerful of Israel's families, but he will lead his army to victory. He will defeat the Philistines in battle."

Not long after, Samuel saw a handsome young man. He and his servant were not local lads: they were searching for some donkeys that had gone missing from their home some distance away.

"He is the one," said God.

Samuel went and anointed the young man with

oil, as a sign of God's choosing. His name was Saul.

Then Samuel called a meeting of the people. He declared the young man king. The crowds cheered.

At first, Saul had no idea what he was meant to do. Then messengers came from a town named Jabesh saying that enemies had attacked them. The condition for peace was horrific: everyone in the town must have one eye blinded.

The enemy king had allowed the Jabeshites one week to consider the offer.

Saul acted swiftly. He called for volunteers to come and join an army. He led attacked the enemy army and won a great victory.

It was the first of many.

DAVID THE SHEPHERD BOY

King Saul proved to be a great warrior. However, he grew to mistrust Samuel. By ignoring Samuel's advice, he ended up disobeying God.

"I want you to choose a new king," said God to Samuel.

"Go to Bethlehem, to the house of a man named Jesse. I have chosen one of his sons to be the next king."

Samuel went. Jesse had many fine sons, but God's choice was the youngest: David, who spent his days out in the pasture looking after the sheep.

It was at this time that King Saul began to feel deeply unsettled by his disagreement with Samuel. He often felt worried and depressed. His servants agreed that music could soothe him.

One of them knew of a talented harp player: it was David himself. He was brought to Saul's court – not to challenge him but to play beautiful music.

When Saul was feeling well, the young man went home to look after the sheep again.

However, his three eldest brothers were part of Saul's army. They were taking part in a bitter war against the Philistines.

One day, David was sent from home to take his brothers a basket of homemade food.

While he was there, the Israelite soldiers lined up on their side of the valley. The Philistines lined up on theirs, ready for battle.

David hurried closer, eager to know how the battle was going. But there was no fighting; instead, a giant of a soldier stepped forward from the ranks of Philistines. He carried sharp iron weapons, and his armour glinted in the sun.

"I am Goliath," he roared. "I challenge you cowards to single combat.

"If you can find a man who can beat me, we will give you the victory."

David's face lit up with excitement.

"I'll fight him!" he declared. "No one should be afraid of a brute of a Philistine!"

David's brothers mocked him, but David would not keep quiet. Soon news of his boast was brought to Saul. He asked to see the brave fighter who had accepted the challenge.

But he was dismayed to see David. "You're just a boy," he said.

"I've fought wild animals and won," said David.

"Goliath is a warrior," argued Saul. "If you really want to go, at least wear my armour."

David tried the armour, but took it off at once.

"It's too heavy," he said. "I'll take my sling. I sling stones at wild animals to chase them away from the sheep. I'm really accurate."

He set off to face Goliath with his shepherd's stick. In the valley he stopped at the stream to pick up five stones.

Goliath glared.

"How dare you?" he snarled. "Do you think you've come to fight a dog?"

"I come in the name of the mighty God of Israel," said David.

Then he whirled his slingshot and aimed a stone at Goliath.

It hit in such a way that the giant fell down.

David had won!

He became the hero of the nation. Already a champion, David proved again and again that he was a fearless fighter.

David's popularity dismayed King Saul. He became so jealous that David had to flee for his life.

For many years he was forced to live as an outlaw. He became a legend among his people. Many who were disappointed with King Saul came to join his band.

David did not seek to defeat him. He waited until he heard the news that Saul had been killed in battle against the Philistines. David knew the time had come to make himself king.

KING DAVID

David did not become king without a fight. His own people, in Judah, welcomed him as their leader. Others, who felt loyal to Saul, resisted his claim.

After a long and bitter struggle, David triumphed over Saul and his followers. He was then able to unite the nation.

With his kingship secure, he went on to defeat the Philistines.

He captured a hilltop fortress and made it his capital city: Jerusalem. He wanted it to be the heart of the nation's worship.

First, he arranged for a tabernacle to be set up in Jerusalem.

Then he arranged a great parade: he led the celebrations as the ark of the covenant was carried on a cart from its humble resting place to Jerusalem.

There he said a prayer of thanksgiving:

How great you are, Lord God.
We, your people, know that you alone are God.
You rescued us from slavery.
You did great things for us, and set us free.
You have promised that we will be your people for ever,
and that my descendants will be kings.

David was sincere in his devotion to God. Yet he could also be tempted to follow his own selfish desires.

One day, from his palace window, he saw a beautiful woman bathing.

He enquired who she was and discovered she was Bathsheba, the wife of Uriah – one of his finest soldiers.

Even so, David wanted to treat Bathsheba as his wife.

He insisted on having his own way. Bathsheba became pregnant from the relationship.

David wanted so much to get rid of Uriah, he arranged for him to be sent into the thick of battle. He was killed.

A prophet, Nathan, came and rebuked David.

David was deeply sorry.

"Forgive me, God," he wept, "because of your great love.

"I would give you anything to win your forgiveness, but there is only one thing you want: a humble and repentant heart."

He could not mend the wrong he had done, but he made Bathsheba his wife and took care of her.

KING SOLOMON

King David had many sons. When he grew old, they began to jostle with each other about who should be the next king.

Nathan, the prophet, went to Bathsheba.

"You must go to David. Remind him of his promise: that your son Solomon would be king after you."

She did so, and David arranged for Solomon to be made king at once.

His final words of advice to him were these:

"Be confident and determined, and do what the Lord your God orders you to do. Obey all his laws

and commands, as written in the Law of Moses, so
that wherever you go you may prosper in everything
you do."

Solomon took his advice to heart. He knew that
he was only king because of God's blessing. He spoke
to God in humble prayer:

"Lord God: give me the wisdom I need to rule
your people with justice and to know the difference
between good and evil."

God answered Solomon's prayer, and he became
famous for his wisdom.

One day, two women came to Solomon. Even as they came to him, they could hardly refrain from clawing each other.

One stepped forward to speak first. "I want you to judge between us," she pleaded.

"We live in the same house. Not long ago we each had a baby. Her child died, and she stole mine while I was sleeping."

"She's lying," shouted the second woman. "The child is mine."

Solomon listened as they shrieked and screamed at one another. Then he gave an order.

"Have the child brought here."

When the infant was brought, he called for a guard with a sword.

"Cut the child in two. Give half to each woman."

"No!" shrieked one of the women. "Give it to her if you must, but don't kill it."

The other woman smiled smugly.

"And now," said Solomon, "give the child to the one who has pleaded for its life. She is the real mother."

The kingdom that David had established prospered. Solomon knew the time was right to complete a plan that David had made: to build a Temple in Jerusalem.

This would replace the tabernacle, which now looked shabby. It would be a magnificent building built of the finest materials: quarried stone, precious wood, and gold.

It would be the place where people could worship God as the laws required.

Its innermost room would be a place to keep the ark of the covenant.

In this way, the Temple would be a reminder that God was the nation's God, and they were God's people.

When the work was complete, Solomon arranged a magnificent ceremony of dedication.

"O God," he prayed, "hear my prayers and the prayers of your people when they face this place and pray. In your home in heaven hear us and forgive us."

For a while, Solomon's rule seemed like a golden age.

The nation was at peace.

It grew wealthy through trading. Merchants from far and wide paid hefty taxes into Solomon's treasury.

Solomon's wealth and wisdom were fabled in distant lands. On one occasion the queen of Sheba herself came many miles to visit Jerusalem. She was impressed by its magnificence.

However, Solomon grew too fond of luxury and self-indulgence.

He forgot to keep God's laws. He chose for himself hundreds of wives. Many of them were foreign. He built shrines for their gods and offered worship there himself.

He also did the very thing that Samuel had warned the nation about, years before. He made it compulsory for many workers to toil on his grand building projects. That left them struggling to make a living for themselves.

When Solomon died, the great families of Israel in the north wanted change. They sent a message to Solomon's son Rehoboam.

"We will only accept you as our king if you life easier for us."

Rehoboam was furious. He not only refused; he threatened to make life even harsher.

The people refused to bow down. The north of the country chose its own king, Jeroboam.

Only Judah remained loyal. A united kingdom split into two.

Two Kingdoms

King Jeroboam of Israel was worried.

The northern tribes of Israel had made him king; but for how long would they stay loyal?

Judah was now a separate kingdom, and Jerusalem was in Judah.

His people would not be able to go and worship in the Temple there.

He chose two places – Dan and Bethel – to be shrines in his own kingdom. In each he placed the statue of a gold bull calf.

"Here are your gods," he declared to the people.

God sent a prophet from Judah up to the kingdom of Israel.

"What you have done is utterly wrong," he declared. "Your kingdom will face ruin because you have turned away from God."

In spite of the warning, Jeroboam did not change his ways. He continued to disregard God's laws about worship.

The kings who came after him were just as faithless. They did not care that they were allowing their people to forget God – the God who had protected them through the years.

Then a new king came to the throne in Israel. His name was Ahab and he was the worst of all.

KING AHAB OF ISRAEL... AND ELIJAH

King Ahab did not care about the God of his people.

He not only married a foreign princess named Jezebel because it was politically wise; he even built shrines to her god, Baal, and the goddess Asherah.

One of God's faithful prophets – a man named Elijah – came with a dire warning.

"God says this: there will be no rain in your kingdom for three years."

Then he turned away and went out to the wild country. There, by a brook, ravens brought Elijah food.

After three years, the lack of rain had caused a famine in Israel. King Ahab was desperate.

It was then that Elijah returned.

"Let us have a contest," said the prophet. "Come to Mount Carmel. There we will build an altar and lay firewood on it to burn the sacrificial offering. Jezebel's prophets must pray to Baal to light the fire, and I will pray to the God of our people.

"The one who answers will show he is the true god."

Ahab agreed. The prophets of Baal came and prayed to their god in a frantic ceremony. No fire came.

Then Elijah ordered servants to drench the altar in water. He prayed to God… and fire came down from heaven. It lit the sodden wood and the offering, and scorched everything around.

The people watched in awe.

"The Lord is God! The Lord alone is God," they cried.

Elijah turned to Ahab.

"And now the rain is coming," he said.

Within a little while the sky filled with clouds. Then came drenching rain.

Ahab went back to his wife, Jezebel, to explain what had happened.

She was furious.

"I'll have that meddling prophet murdered!" she screamed.

Once again Elijah had to flee. It was some considerable time later that he dared return. He went to Ahab's court for the briefest meeting: to warn that God condemned both Ahab and Jezebel. Their lives would end in disaster.

It was not long before Ahab died.

Elisha

When Elijah grew old, he chose a man named Elisha to be the next prophet in Israel. Elisha saw the older prophet taken up to heaven in a chariot of fire.

God gave Elisha the power to work miracles. It earned him great respect among the people of Israel.

At the time, the nation was at war with Syria, to the north. In one of their raids, the Syrians captured prisoners and made them slaves. That was how a young girl became a servant to the wife of a Syrian general: Naaman.

One day, Naaman was stricken with a dreadful skin disease. He could find no cure.

The servant girl tried to comfort Naaman's wife. "If only my master could go to the prophet in Israel, Elisha," she soothed. "I am quite sure he would be able to cure him."

When Naaman heard of this, he asked his king for permission to go to Israel, in spite of the war.

Elisha agreed to help. When Naaman arrived, Elisha sent his servant to tell him to wash in the River Jordan seven times.

Naaman was angry at the request. "Does that man think his filthy river water is the cure? We have better rivers in Syria!"

His servants tried to calm him. "Why not try?" they said. "It's such an easy thing to do."

Grudgingly, Naaman clambered down into the River Jordan and washed seven times. At once, he was healed.

Still the war against Syria continued.

"Why are we unable to defeat the people of Israel?" the king of Syria complained.

"They have the prophet Elisha to guide them," replied his servants. "He advises the king on how to conduct the campaign."

On one occasion the Syrians had laid siege to the Israelite city of Samaria. Inside the walls the people were starving.

"Do not be afraid," Elisha told the king. "By tomorrow the people will have all the food they need."

No one believed him.

It so happened that there were four men who had a dreaded skin disease. They were forced to live outside the city walls so they could not infect others. They too were starving.

"There's no point trying to get into the city," they agreed, "because there's no food there.

"We'd do better raiding the Syrian camp for food. We might get killed in the attempt, but that would be better than waiting to die of hunger."

Warily they made their way to the enemy camp. To their astonishment they found it deserted. Food and treasure were there for the taking.

God had worked a miracle: he had made the Syrians hear a noise that sounded like a mighty army. The Syrians feared the worst – that other nations had joined with Israel to defeat them.

The entire Syrian army had panicked and fled.

When the people of Israel heard the news, they came into the camp and took all the food they needed.

THE ASSYRIAN MENACE

God worked miracles in Israel through Elisha. However, the rulers of the land continued to be as faithless as Ahab.

God told Elisha to go and anoint another man to be king: a fearless army officer named Jehu.

Then, as Elisha instructed, Jehu drove his chariot to the royal city. Jezebel was now the queen mother and she watched him arrive.

Jehu brought his chariot to a halt. He shouted up at the window, "Who is on my side?"

Jezebel's own servants had grown weary of her wicked cruelty. They threw her to the ground.

Jehu set about reforming the nation. He forbade the worship of Baal. He reminded everyone to be loyal to their God.

His resolve proved short lived. All too soon he, like the other kings of Israel, forgot his promises.

Once again the nation turned away from God and one bad king followed another.

All the while, another nation was growing more powerful: Assyria, to the north of Syria. Its army was unstoppable. Its many victories enabled the Assyrians to enlarge their empire.

The day came when the Assyrian emperor led his armies into the great city of Israel: Samaria.

It was God who allowed this crushing defeat. The people of Israel had not kept their side of the covenant agreement.

They were forced to go and live in other lands.

The Assyrians forced another defeated people to make their home in Israel.

These new arrivals – the Samaritans – brought their own gods with them. They also asked to learn about the God of Israel. From that day to the time of Jesus, their worship of God was mixed up with their other customs.

HEZEKIAH AND THE SIEGE OF JERUSALEM

The Assyrian army had defeated the kingdom of Israel. It swept down through the kingdom of Judah, and laid siege to Jerusalem.

The king, Hezekiah, was desperate. He asked for the advice of a prophet named Isaiah.

"Don't be afraid," was the prophet's message. "God says this:

" 'I will protect the city because of the promise I made to King David.' "

That night, a mystery illness swept through the Assyrian camp. Thousands died in just a few hours.

The remnant of the army left for home. Jerusalem was safe.

THE STORY OF JONAH

Far and wide the news of the Assyrians spread. They were the cruellest, most wicked nation on earth.

God went and spoke to a prophet named Jonah.

"I want you to go to Nineveh, the great city of the Assyrians. Tell them I have seen how wicked they are.

"Tell them they must change their ways, or I will punish them."

Jonah was dismayed. He hated the Assyrians for their wickedness. He *wanted* them punished.

He hurried down to a seaport. He found a boat that was ready to sail far, far away – as far from Nineveh as anyone could get.

He got on board. As night fell, he settled down to sleep, feeling content to have made his escape.

But God had seen what Jonah was doing. God sent a terrible storm that tossed the boat among towering waves.

"This is no normal storm," cried the sailors. "Someone has displeased their god! That is the only explanation!"

Jonah was forced to confess. He was running away from God.

"Throw me into the sea," he declared to the sailors. "There is no other way to save yourselves."

They did so, and the sea fell calm. Jonah sank into the deep, dark water.

Then a great cavernous mouth opened. A great sea creature had swallowed him whole.

In desperation, Jonah said a prayer. "I am sorry I disobeyed you, God," he wailed.

At God's command, the sea creature swam close to shore. It belched Jonah onto the beach.

The bedraggled prophet hurried to Nineveh.

There he walked up and down the streets. "Repent of your wicked ways," he cried. "If you do not, God will punish you."

The people of Nineveh heard what he said. They were deeply sorry. They changed their ways.

Jonah went a little way off and sulked. "I knew that would happen," he complained.

The sun was hot. God caused a plant to grow and spread its leaves for shade.

Jonah was delighted.

Then God sent a worm. It ate the stem, and the plant died.

Jonah was furious. "That's so unfair," he raged at God. "I loved that plant!"

"Did you?" said God. "Then you should understand me better.

"I care about Nineveh: its people, and its animals."

THE DEFEAT OF JUDAH

In the kingdom of Judah there had been good kings and bad kings.

Some were as faithless as those of Israel. Others were loyal to their God.

Famous among these was Josiah. When he was king, he ordered repairs to be done to God's Temple. As the builders set about their work, they found a scroll.

A priest brought it to Josiah and read it aloud.

The king was dismayed at what he heard.

"These are the laws we were given to live by," he declared. "There is so much we have forgotten!"

He ordered that the shrines to foreign gods be torn down. He declared that the nation must celebrate Passover in Jerusalem. It was a festival like no other.

Not many years after he died, a new threat arose. King Nebuchadnezzar of Babylon had become the most feared ruler in all the world – defeating even Assyria.

He demanded that the people of Judah accept defeat. He wanted the land to be part of his empire.

For a while, the rulers of Judah tried to reach a settlement. In the end their efforts came to nothing.

Jerusalem was attacked and defeated.

The city and its Temple were burned.

Many of the leading people were taken to live in exile.

The ark of the covenant disappeared and was never seen again.

The people of Judah lamented their wrongdoing and the disaster that it had brought them.

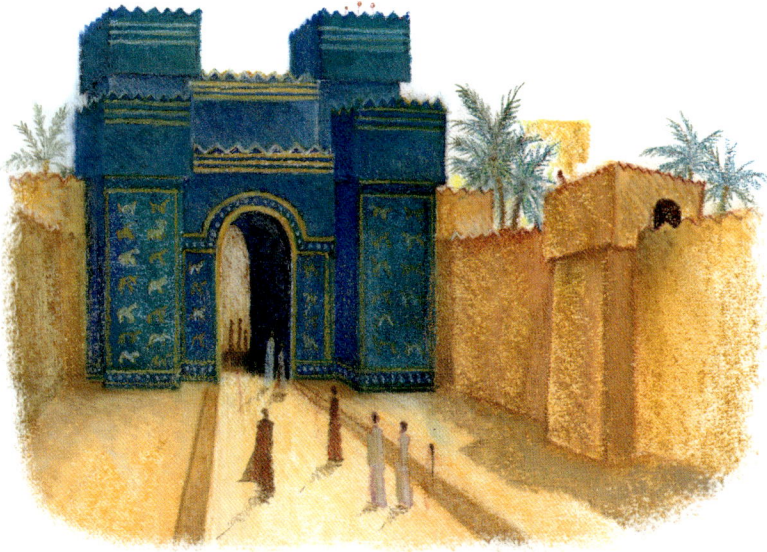

THE JEWISH PEOPLE

King Nebuchadnezzar ruled his empire from the mighty city of Babylon. The treasures captured in war had brought great wealth. Babylon's splendid buildings were among the wonders of the world.

Yet, for the people of Judah, taken there as exiles, it was a bleak place. The great gateway dedicated to the goddess Ishtar reminded them that they were captives of a people who did not worship God.

They did their best to cling on to their traditions and their faith.

It became the custom to meet on the sabbath day of rest. They did not have a place of worship to call their own, so they met on the riverbank.

There, those that were wise taught them the old stories of their people.

They taught them the laws that God had given so long ago.

As a nation they were determined not to forget who they were: the people of God.

Even the residents of Babylon were intrigued by these exiles from Judah. They called them the Jews.

EZEKIEL AND THE GOOD SHEPHERD

The Jews who lived in Babylon often felt downcast.

A prophet named Ezekiel brought them words of hope.

"God says this: 'I will take care of my people as a shepherd takes care of his sheep.

"'I will bring them back from the places to which they have been scattered.

"'I will lead them back to the mountains and streams of Israel.

" 'I will let them graze in safety in the mountain meadows and the green pastures.

" 'I will look for those that are lost, bring back those that wander off, bandage those that are hurt, and heal those that are sick.

" 'I will give them a king like my servant David to be their one shepherd, and he will take care of them.

" 'You, my sheep, the flock that I feed, are my people, and I am your God.' "

THE FIERY FURNACE

When King Nebuchadnezzar attacked Jerusalem, he chose the finest young men to be his prisoners.

He took them to Babylon and had them trained to work in his government. A young man named Daniel impressed him greatly. So did three other Jews, to whom he gave Babylonian names:

Shadrach, Meshach, and Abednego.

One day, King Nebuchadnezzar had a golden statue set up of the plain outside the city.

He sent an order:

"I want all the officials in my government to come to a ceremony. I want to dedicate the statue of the Babylonian god."

When everyone had assembled, a herald called his message.

"People of all nations, races and languages: the orchestra is about to play. When you hear the music, you are to bow down to the king's statue.

"If you do not obey, you will be thrown into a blazing, fiery furnace."

The music played. Everyone bowed down.

Except for three:

Shadrach, Meshach, and Abednego.

When King Nebuchadnezzar heard of their disobedience, he flew into a rage.

"Bring them here!" he cried. "I demand to know why they will not obey my orders."

The young men stood boldly in front of him to answer.

"Your Majesty, we will not try to defend ourselves.

"If the God whom we serve is able to save us from the blazing furnace, then he will.

"But even if he doesn't, we will not worship your god. We will not bow down to your golden statue."

King Nebuchadnezzar lost his temper completely.

"Make the fire seven times hotter," he thundered. "Tie those scoundrels up and throw them into the flames."

Everything was done as he required.

The king watched with a grim smile. Suddenly he leaped to his feet.

"What's that I see? Those men are no longer bound. They're simply dancing around.

"And there's someone else in there... someone who looks like an angel."

Terrified, the king marched to the door of the furnace and shouted.

"Shadrach, Meshach, and Abednego: come out!"

The young men came out smiling. They were not in least bit harmed.

Nebuchadnezzar was humbled. He made this pronouncement:

"I declare that the God of Shadrach, Meshach, and Abednego is the greatest of all gods. There is none who can rescue his people like this."

THE WRITING ON THE WALL

Daniel was one of the Jews whom Nebuchadnezzar trained to work in his government. He proved to be intelligent and reliable.

In time, he became the king's trusted advisor.

Then a new king came to power: Nebuchadnezzar's son Belshazzar. He was something of a wastrel. He didn't know or care about Daniel because he did not concern himself with good government.

One night he was having a riotous party. He and his guests were drinking far too much wine. They sang noisy praises to the gods of their nation.

Suddenly a ghostly hand appeared.

It was just a hand… disembodied. It began writing.

Belshazzar turned pale. He called for his advisors to read the message. None could do so.

The queen mother heard the noise and came to find out what the problem was. Her response to it was swift.

"You should go and ask your father's chief advisor, Daniel. He understands many mysteries."

Belshazzar sent for Daniel, and he read the words:

MENE, MENE, TEKEL, PARSIN

"The words mean number, weight, division," Daniel explained.

"God has numbered the days of your kingdom.

"God has weighed your character and declares you a lightweight.

"God will divide your kingdom and give it to the Medes and Persians."

That same night, Belshazzar was killed. Darius the Mede became king.

DANIEL AND THE LIONS

King Darius needed good people to work in his government. He ruled a great many different nations, and he needed people who were trustworthy and efficient.

It was no surprise that he gave Daniel one of the most senior jobs. When he saw Daniel's excellent work, he gave him the most senior job of all.

That made other people furiously jealous.

They gathered to whisper their complaints to one another. Then they hatched a plan.

They went to the king.

"Your Majesty Darius," they began. "May you live for ever.

"We, your government officials, have agreed on a new law. it is designed to make sure that everyone, whatever their background, is completely loyal.

"For thirty days no one must appeal to anyone in heaven or earth for anything... except from you.

"If they do, they will be thrown into a pit of lions.

"This law will be a law of the Medes and Persians: one that cannot be changed."

The king approved the idea readily. He passed the law without any delay.

The conspirators went to spy on Daniel.

"We know his daily routine!" they laughed. "We know when he'll be at the window of his room. He'll face Jerusalem, the city of his homeland Judah, and say prayers to his God."

Daniel had always remained faithful to God. It wasn't long before he came to the window and began saying prayers.

The conspirators hurried to betray Daniel to the king.

"The man has quite clearly paid no attention whatsoever to your law," they told him.

Darius was unconcerned. "The law wasn't to check up on Daniel," he said. "I know he's completely loyal."

The conspirators glowered. "It's the law," they reminded the king. "The law of the Medes and Persians, one that cannot be changed.

"You must abide by it."

Darius was trapped. He knew he had no choice. Reluctantly he gave orders for Daniel to be thrown to the lions.

"May your God save you," he whispered, as Daniel was led to a certain death.

Darius passed a sleepless night. Nothing could distract him from fretting about Daniel.

In the morning he went to the pit.

Anxiously he called out: "Daniel – are you there?"

"May Your Majesty live for ever," replied Daniel.

"God sent an angel to protect me. The lions never even opened their mouths.

"God knows I was innocent and have never done you any wrong."

Darius was delighted.

He ordered Daniel to be hauled to safety.

He sent a message to be taken to every part of the empire.

"From now on, everyone must respect Daniel's God.

"He is the greatest and most powerful God of all."

As for the conspirators... they were given the punishment they had wanted for Daniel.

QUEEN ESTHER

The Persian empire was prosperous. Many Jews moved to different towns and cities within it. There they could live in peace and make a good living.

In the reign of King Xerxes, a great celebration was held in the city of Susa. One night, the king got drunk at a party.

"I know a beautiful woman who could come and entertain us," he said to his guests.

He sent for the queen. She refused to be treated in this way and did not come.

In a temper, Xerxes sent her into exile.

The king asked his officials to search the empire for a beautiful woman to be his next queen. They chose Esther: a young Jewish woman.

She was an orphan and had been raised by a cousin, Mordecai. "Don't tell anyone in the palace you're Jewish," he warned. "Jews have many enemies."

Esther did as Mordecai advised. He was wise and well respected. He had also proved himself to be loyal to the king.

Mordecai had even foiled a conspiracy against Xerxes.

However, it was at this time that the king chose a man named Haman to be his chief advisor. He was jealous of Mordecai. His hatred for the man turned into a hatred for all the Jews.

He issued an order in the king's name. He set the date for a massacre – a day when it would be legal for anyone in the empire to turn on their Jewish neighbours and kill them.

Mordecai sent a message to Esther.

"You have to do something," he told her. "Only you can save your people."

The task was daunting. Esther knew she could not go to the king unasked. If she did, he had the right to order her execution. He hadn't asked to see her for many days.

Bravely she put on her loveliest gown. Bravely she went to the king. To her relief, he welcomed her.

"What favour do you want?" he asked.

"I want to invite you to a dinner party," she said. "And please bring Haman too."

The evening went very well. "I do have a request," she told the king, "but please – let me invite you a second time before I ask it."

The invitation to second party cheered Haman. But then, as was going home, he saw Mordecai. He remembered how much he hated him.

His wife had an idea. "You could so easily get Xerxes to order his execution," she said. "Arrange to have the gallows built as soon as morning comes."

Haman was delighted to see the work begun as he set off for the palace. But Xerxes had a different plan for Mordecai's future.

"I've just been reminded of how Mordecai saved me from an assassination plot," he told Haman. "I want you to take him on a parade of honour this very day."

Haman could not refuse. Honouring Mordecai left him in a furious temper. He might even have forgotten the second dinner party, except that servants came to fetch him.

As the evening came to a close, Esther made her request to the king.

"Please: put a stop to the massacre of the Jews. They are my people."

The king was dismayed. "Who has ordered such a terrible thing?" he asked.

"That man there," Esther replied. And she pointed at Haman.

The king left the room. When he returned, he saw Haman clutching at his wife, pleading with her.

"You impudent wretch," he cried. "I'll have you punished for this."

Haman was hung on the gallows he had built for Mordecai.

The Jews were given the right to defend themselves. Esther had saved her people.

THE LAND OF THE JEWS

The Babylonians had taken many people from Judah into exile.

When the Persians took control of the empire, they had a new plan: exiles from every nation were given permission to return home.

So it was that a band of Jews set out for their homeland, eager to rebuild Jerusalem.

The early years were hard. Other nations had been settled in Judah. They resented having to make room for those who were returning, and they made life difficult for them.

The Jews persisted. God inspired prophets to speak words of encouragement. In time, a modest Temple was built; it had nothing of the splendour of Solomon's Temple, but it was a place to worship God.

Some years later, news of the state of Jerusalem was brought to a man named Nehemiah. He was a Jew who worked as a butler to the emperor.

Nehemiah was dismayed at what he heard. At once he asked for permission to go and help his people.

His request was granted. Nehemiah made the long journey to Jerusalem. There he took charge of rebuilding the city walls.

At the same time, a priest named Ezra came to the city. He held open-air assemblies where he taught the people about the Law and their traditions.

This in itself gave the people a sense of hope for the future. So did the words of prophets, reminding the people of God's promises:

Arise, Jerusalem, and shine like the sun;
The glory of the Lord is shining on you!
Other nations will be covered by darkness,
But on you the light of the Lord will shine;
The brightness of his presence will be with you.
Nations will be drawn to your light,
And kings to the dawning of your new day.

But disappointment and defeat were just around the corner.

First came the Greek invasion. The Greeks defeated the Persians and put themselves in charge of a vast empire. They captured Jerusalem and put their own gods in the Temple.

A Jew named Judas Maccabeus led a successful rebellion, and restored the Temple; but the people were not truly free.

Then the Romans came and defeated the Greeks.

They chose who should rule the land of the Jews.

The people had nothing to turn to but their stories and their laws.

They met each sabbath in their meetings places, the synagogues.

They put their faith in the words of the prophets, who told of God's promise:

One day, God would send another king like David: a messiah.

THE BIRTH OF JESUS

In the time of the Roman empire, a man named
Herod was made king in Jerusalem.

He was eager to impress people with displays
of his wealth and power. He organized many fine
building projects. Among them was a splendid new
Temple in Jerusalem.

One day, it was the turn of a priest named
Zechariah to burn the incense on the altar there. An
angel appeared.

"Don't be afraid," said the angel.

"I bring good news. Your wife, Elizabeth, is going to have a baby. You must dedicate him to God.

"He will grow up to be a prophet. His preaching will inspire people to live as God wants. He will prepare the nation for the coming of God's messiah."

"That can't be possible," Zechariah protested. "My wife, Elizabeth, and I are too old now to be parents!"

"Do you not believe me?" asked the angel. "Then believe this: you will not be able to speak until my words come true."

From that moment on Zechariah found he was unable to utter a word. Elizabeth was as puzzled as anyone when he returned home.

Not long after, however, she became pregnant.

MARY AND THE ANGEL

In the village of Nazareth, in the region of Galilee, lived a woman named Mary.

She was looking forward to marrying a man named Joseph. Her life was ordinary, happy, and calm.

Then God sent the angel Gabriel to Nazareth with a message for her.

Mary was startled.

"Don't be afraid," said the angel. "God has chosen you and has greatly blessed you.

"God wants you to be the mother of his Son. You will name him Jesus.

"He will be a king, like King David of old, and his kingdom will never end."

"That can't be true," protested Mary. "I'm not yet married."

"What I say will come true," replied the angel, "because God will make it come true. For this reason the child will be called the Son of God."

Mary hardly hesitated. "I will do as God wants," she replied.

Not long after, Mary decided to visit her cousin: Elizabeth, Zechariah's wife.

The two hugged each other for joy.

"My baby is dancing inside me!" laughed Elizabeth. "It's as if he too is celebrating your news. Truly, God has blessed you and God will bless your child."

Mary sang aloud. "I'm so happy!

"God has done wonderful things for me.

"And he has kept the promise he made to our people, to take care of them for ever!"

THE BIRTH OF JOHN

The time came for Elizabeth to have her baby. Her friends and neighbours were thrilled for her.

"Welcome baby Zechariah!" they cooed.

"Actually, his name is John," said Elizabeth.

"No!" they exclaimed. "The firstborn boy takes the same name as his father."

Zechariah asked for a writing tablet.

"His name is John," he wrote.

From that moment, Zechariah was able to speak again.

"Let us all praise God," he cried. "He is faithful and keeps his promises to his people, to bless them.

"And you, my son – you will prepare the way for his coming, for the bright dawn of salvation."

THE BABY IN THE MANGER

"Mary is expecting a baby."

The news that was the talk of Nazareth made Joseph sad. Mary's baby wasn't his baby. Perhaps he should call off their wedding.

In a dream, an angel spoke to him.

"God has chosen you too, Joseph. God wants you to take care of Mary and her baby."

It was at this time that the Roman emperor Caesar Augustus sent an order. He wanted everyone to go to their hometown, to register as taxpayers.

Joseph went to see Mary.

"You know my family is descended from that of King David," he began, "and that means my hometown is Bethlehem.

"Let us go there together, for we are going to be a family!"

Mary agreed.

Even though she was heavily pregnant, she made the journey of many miles from Nazareth to Bethlehem.

There was dismal news on their arrival: there was no room at the inn.

They had to shelter in a stable. There, Mary's baby was born. She swaddled him in cloths and laid him in a manger.

On the hillsides nearby some shepherds huddled around a fire.

Their sheep were gathered inside a low-walled sheepfold. Bleating rippled through the chill night air.

"Nothing gets better with the Romans in charge, does it?" they grumbled. "Bethlehem is full tonight: full of visitors from far and wide come to put their names on the tax register. Money to make the emperor rich – that's what it is."

"And we'll be overcharged by the scoundrels that collect the taxes," added another. "It's daylight robbery, paying your taxes these days."

"Now if we were an independent country," began another…

"… and a king like David would take charge…"

Suddenly the dark sky turned bright.

An angel appeared, and the shepherds shrank back in fear.

"Don't be afraid," said the angel. "I bring good news. Tonight, in Bethlehem – the town of King David – a baby has been born.

"He is God's promised king, the messiah, the Christ.

"Go up to the town and see for yourselves. You will find the baby wrapped in swaddling clothes and lying in a manger."

Then a multitude of heaven's angels appeared. They sang praises to God in highest heaven.

As suddenly as the angels had appeared, they vanished into the dark sky.

"Let's go to Bethlehem!" agreed the shepherds.

They went, and found Mary and Joseph and baby Jesus, just as the angel had said.

Mary listened carefully to all they said about the angels. That night would be a memory for her to treasure for always.

THE WISE MEN AND THEIR GIFTS

In lands far to the east, those who were learned and wise studied the night skies; they watched the patterns of the stars as they floated through the sky.

One day, a small group of these stargazers noticed something new: a bright star they had not seen before, and that was moving at remarkable speed through the heavens.

"It must be the sign that a king has been born," they agreed. "Let us follow it, to find the king and pay him tribute."

The star led them to the land of the Jews, and to Jerusalem. There the men began asking about a newborn king.

Soon it seemed that everyone in the city had heard about their question. In his palace, Herod heard the news and frowned in anger.

"I am king of the Jews," he reminded his advisors. "Now fetch the priests. They and the people cling to some prophesy or other – that God has promised to send a messiah. I need to know more."

The priests were eager to explain. "The Scriptures are very clear about it," they explained. "The messiah will be born in Bethlehem."

Herod summoned the wise men and asked them many questions. Then he sent them to Bethlehem.

"Go and find the child," he said. "When you have done so, come and tell me where he is."

The wise men headed out on the road to Bethlehem. Light from the star lit the way.

It stopped over one particular house in Bethlehem. The men went inside and found Mary and Jesus.

They brought out their tribute gifts: gold, frankincense, and myrrh.

That night, in a dream, an angel spoke to them.

"Don't go back to Herod," the angel warned. "He intends to harm the child."

They took the warning seriously. The following day the men did not go back to Herod in Jerusalem. They chose a different road for their journey home.

In a dream, an angel also spoke to Joseph.

"Hurry, wake up! King Herod has heard of a newborn king in Bethlehem. He will send soldiers to kill him.

"You must wake Mary, and together take the child to faraway Egypt. Stay there until it is safe for you to return."

JESUS IN THE TEMPLE

The years went by. Joseph heard the news that King Herod had died. He took his family back to Nazareth.

There, Jesus grew up with the other boys. He learned to be a carpenter, like Joseph. He went to school with the other boys and learned to read the special books of the Jewish people: the Scriptures, which contained the stories of his people, the Law, and the sayings of the prophets.

When he was twelve, Jesus joined his parents on the pilgrimage to Jerusalem, for the Passover festival. They remembered the covenant that God had made with his people so long ago, in the time of Moses.

When it was over, the group all set out together. They had gone a whole day before Mary realized something awful: Jesus was not with them. He was not with anyone from Nazareth. He was simply missing!

She and Joseph rushed back to Jerusalem. For three days they hunted high and low for Jesus.

Then they found him. He was in the Temple courtyard, talking earnestly with some of the most important teachers there.

He was discussing the Jewish faith, and the meaning of the Scriptures. The teachers looked very impressed with what he was saying.

Mary rushed up to him.

"Where have you been? Why did you do this to us?" she wanted to know.

Jesus looked surprised.

"Didn't you know where I was?" he asked. "I had to be in my Father's house."

Then he returned with them to Nazareth, and grew up an obedient son.

JESUS THE TEACHER

Elizabeth's son, John, grew up to be a preacher. He lived out in the wild country, and he looked like a prophet from days gone by, with his uncut hair and rough brown cloak.

Even so, many people came to listen to him.

"It is time for people to repent. Change your ways and live as God wants."

Many were eager to declare they would make a fresh start. He baptized them in the River Jordan.

One day, Jesus came and asked to be baptized.

"You don't need to make a fresh start," retorted John. "You have not done anything to repent of."

Jesus insisted.

John lowered Jesus beneath the water and then lifted him up.

God's Holy Spirit came and landed on Jesus in the form of a dove.

A voice from heaven spoke aloud.

"You are my own dear Son. I am pleased with you."

After that, Jesus went away to the wild country. He knew it was time to begin God's work. For forty days and days he spent time thinking and praying. He ate nothing.

Then the devil came to tempt him from his calling.

"If you are God's Son, you could work a miracle. You could turn these stones into bread."

"No," said Jesus. "The Scriptures say, 'People cannot live on bread alone.'"

Later, the devil showed Jesus all the kingdoms of the world. "I can give you these," said the Devil. "You just have to worship me."

"No, said Jesus. "The Scriptures say, 'Worship the Lord your God and serve only him.'"

A third time the devil came. He took him to the highest point of the Temple in Jerusalem.

"Prove you are God's Son," he said. "Throw yourself down. God's own angels will come to save you."

"No, no, and no," said Jesus. "The Scripture says, 'Do not put the Lord your God to the test.'"

The devil went away. Jesus returned to the region of Galilee, and to Nazareth.

JESUS IN THE SYNAGOGUE

It was a sabbath day in Nazareth. Everyone had gathered in the synagogue. It was Jesus' turn to read from the Scriptures. That day's reading was from the book of the prophet Isaiah.

Jesus read these words:

The Spirit of the Lord is upon me,
because he has chosen me to bring good news to the poor...
... to announce that the time has come when God will
save his people.

Everyone in the synagogue was staring at Jesus. He added quietly:

"These words have come true today, as you heard them being read."

His words caused uproar. "Are you saying you're God's prophet?" people challenged him. "How arrogant! How ridiculous! How wrong!"

Amid the noise and confusion, Jesus slipped away. He went to Capernaum on the shores of Lake Galilee.

He was welcomed into the home of a young fisherman: Simon.

Simon's mother-in-law was unwell. With a touch, Jesus healed her.

News of his power to heal spread quickly. People in need of healing came from far and wide. He healed those who were sick in body and those who were troubled in their mind.

Soon he was being welcomed to preach in synagogues all over Galilee.

JESUS AND HIS DISCIPLES

One day, Jesus went down to the lake shore in Capernaum. People were crowding round him, hoping to hear him preach.

Some fishermen watched him arriving. They were cleaning their nets after a night's fishing.

Jesus got into the boat that belonged to his friend Simon. From there he preached to the crowds.

When he had finished, he went up to Simon.

"Go back out in your boat," he told him. "Let down your nets for an enormous catch."

Simon shook his head. "We were fishing all night. We caught nothing."

Jesus went on looking at him.

"If you want me to, I can," said Simon.

He pushed his boat into deeper water and let down the nets.

At once they were so full of fish he could not haul them in. He had to call to his friends for help.

When they were back on shore, Simon fell on his knees in front of Jesus.

"Just leave me to my ordinary life," he pleaded.

"But I want you to come and help me in my work," replied Jesus. "You will help draw people into my kingdom."

Four fishermen joined Jesus that day: Simon, whom he named Peter, and his brother Andrew; James, and his brother John. They were the first disciples.

On another occasion, Jesus was in the marketplace.

He saw a tax collector: he was sitting in his booth collecting the money from the people. Some was what the Romans demanded; some was for his own pay.

He job made him an outcast. No one thought of a tax collector as godly.

Jesus spoke to him simply: "Follow me," he said.

The man got up at once and followed him.

He threw a party to celebrate. Jesus and his disciples ate and drank with tax collectors and other outcasts.

The most religious people in the time of Jesus were the synagogue teachers, the rabbis. Some of them belonged to a group known as Pharisees. They prided themselves on their holy lives.

They saw Jesus and disapproved.

"How can Jesus claim to be a good teacher?" they grumbled. "If he were, he wouldn't mix with that rabble."

Jesus knew what they were thinking.

"I haven't come to preach my message to respectable people," he said. "I have come to call outcasts back to God."

Jesus became increasingly popular with ordinary people. Crowds flocked to hear him.

Jesus chose seven more people to help him in his work: twelve disciples.

Simon Peter and his brother Andrew; James and his brother John; Matthew the tax collector; Philip, Bartholomew, Thomas, another James, Thaddaeus, another Simon, and Judas Iscariot.

Living as God wants

One day, Jesus was out among the hills of Galilee. A crowd gathered, and he preached to them.

"Happy are those who know they don't understand spiritual things," he said. "The kingdom of heaven belongs to them.

"Happy are those who want more than anything to live as God wants. God will satisfy their longing.

"Happy are those who are merciful to others. God will be merciful to them."

The people hung on his every word as he continued speaking.

"Don't think I have come to do away with the old teaching: the laws that Moses gave our people and the words of the prophets.

"I have come to make their teaching come true.

"If you want to live as God requires, you must go beyond the Law.

"You know the old saying about revenge: an eye for an eye and a tooth for a tooth. It's a reminder to keep revenge balanced and fair.

"Now I'm telling you not to seek revenge at all. If someone slaps you on one cheek, let them slap you on the other.

"If a Roman soldier demands that you carry his pack one mile, offer to carry it for a second mile.

"You know the old saying about how to treat others – love your friends, hate your enemies.

"Now I'm telling you to love your enemies as much as your friends.

"God's blessings of sun and rain are for good people and bad people alike.

"You must imitate God in the way you treat people: you must do what is kind and helpful to good and bad people alike.

"And when you pray, do not make it an excuse to show off. There are some who like to stand up and pray on street corners.

"You must go to a quiet place. Go to your room, perhaps, and close the door.

"Don't make your prayers long and complicated. Your Father in heaven knows what you need before you ask. Instead, say this:

Our Father in heaven;

May your holy name be honoured;

may your kingdom come;

may your will be done on earth as it is in heaven.

Give us today the food we need.

Forgive us the wrongs we have done,

as we forgive the wrongs that others have done to us.

Do not bring us to hard testing,

but keep us safe from the Evil One.

"No one can be a loyal servant of two masters. In the same way, you can't be a loyal to God and still be ordered about by money.

"Don't worry about food. Look at the wild birds. They don't sow seeds or gather a harvest. Yet God provides all they need.

"Don't worry about clothes either. Look at the wild flowers. They don't spin thread or weave cloth, but their fragile petals are lovelier that the costliest robes. King Solomon himself never had such finery.

"Instead, make it your aim to live as God wants. Live as members of God's kingdom.

"God knows what you need, and God will provide for you."

THE KINGDOM OF GOD

When Jesus preached, he often told stories.

"Once," he said, "a man went to his field to sow seed. He flung it from his basket by the handful.

"Some seed fell on the path. Birds swooped down and ate it.

"Some fell on rocky ground. The seeds sprouted but their roots did not grow deep. The seedlings wilted in the sun.

"Some fell among thorn bushes. The seeds produced young plants but they were soon choked.

"Some seed fell on good ground. It grew into fine young plants that produced a harvest."

Then the story was over. "Listen to its message," said Jesus, "if you have the ears to hear."

Later, when the crowds had gone, Jesus' disciples came to him.

"Why do you talk in parables?" they asked. "These stories leave us puzzled."

"I tell stories to help people understand more about God's kingdom," Jesus replied. "Only some will grasp it.

"You are in a position that even the prophets would long for: you have me here with you to explain!

"This is what the parable of the sower means:

"The seed that falls on the path stands for people who hear the message about God's kingdom. In no time at all, the Devil comes and snatches it from them.

"The seed that falls on rocky ground stands for those who start out full of enthusiasm for my message. However, when obeying my teaching gets tough, they give up.

"The seed that falls among thorns stands for those who hear the message and begin to live by it. Then everyday cares and worries get in the way.

"The seed that falls on good soil stands for those who hear my message and understand it: really, truly, deeply.

"Their changed lives yield a harvest of good things."

PARABLES OF THE KINGDOM

"The kingdom of God is like this," said Jesus. "A woman takes a pinch of yeast and mixes it into her dough. The yeast is enough to make the whole batch of dough rise.

"The kingdom of God is like this," said Jesus. "Someone takes a tiny mustard seed and sows it in the ground. It grows into an enormous tree. All the birds of the air come and nest in its branches.

"The kingdom of God is like this," said Jesus. "A man is digging in a field. His spade strikes something hard; he scrabbles around and finds it is buried treasure.

"At once he covers up the hole. Then he goes and sells all he has so he can buy the field. The treasure is his!

"Or you might say the kingdom is like this:

"Someone is a collector of fine pearls. One day they come across a pearl that is finer than any they have ever seen.

"They go and sell all of their lesser pearls so they can have the one that is just perfect."

Belonging to God's kingdom

Who can enter the kingdom of God?

The people who came to listen to Jesus were from many different backgrounds. One day the crowd included many tax collectors and other outcasts.

The rabbis were full of contempt. "It's just as we've noticed before," they agreed.

"Jesus mixes with the wrong kinds of people. So much for his obedience to God's Law!"

Jesus told them this parable:

"Suppose you had a hundred sheep," he said. "Suppose one went missing.

"What would you do?

"The answer is quite clear: you would leave the ninety-nine who were safe in the pasture and go and find the lost sheep.

"When you found it, you would pick it up gently and carry it home.

"Once it was returned to the flock you would call out to your neighbours, 'Come and celebrate with me! I found the sheep that was lost!'

"In the same way, when even one wrongdoer comes back to God, all the angels sing."

Jesus continued speaking.

"There was once a man who had two sons. One day, the younger came to him with a request.

" 'I will inherit my share of your farm when you die. But I'll be old then. I want it now.'

"The father was sad, but he let his son have his way.

"The young man took the money and went off to a city far away. He bought luxuries and threw parties. In no time at all, his money was gone.

"Then a famine struck. The harvests had failed and the price of food went up.

"The young man had to go and get a job.

"The only work he could find was on another man's farm. He had to look after the pigs.

"He was so hungry, he was tempted to eat their food.

"Then he came to his senses.

" 'My father's servants eat better than this!' he said to himself. 'I shall go back to my father, say I'm sorry, and ask to be hired as a servant.'

"He set out on the long journey home.

"He was still some way off when he heard someone running. It was his father, running to greet him and hug him close.

" 'I want to say how sorry I am,' began the young man. 'I did wrong to you and to God. I would like to be a servant on your farm.'

"The father wasn't listening. 'Hurry,' he called to his servants. 'I want you to get this boy washed and properly dressed.

" 'And the kitchen servants – I want a feast prepared.

" 'We're going to have a party to celebrate his homecoming.'

"As the sun began to dip low, the party started. The sound of noisy music floated over the fields. The older son heard it as he returned from a hard day's work.

"'What's going on?' he asked a servant.

"'It's a party,' came the reply. 'Your brother has come home. Your father is celebrating in style.'

"The older brother was furious. 'Well, I'm not going to join in!' he exclaimed.

"His father came out to talk to him. 'You never did anything like this for me!' said the son. 'I've been loyal. I've worked hard. And what thanks do I get? None!'

"The father looked concerned. 'Everything I have is yours,' he said. 'But we have to celebrate your brother's return. Once he was lost. Now he is found.'"

One day a young man came to Jesus with a question.

"Teacher," he said, "what must I do to have eternal life?"

"You know the commandments," replied Jesus.

"I do!" said the young man. "I have obeyed them since I was young."

Jesus looked directly at the man. "There is one more thing you must do," he said. "Sell all your riches, then come and follow me."

"Really?" asked the young man. "Well, I'll need to think about that."

Jesus shook his head as the young man walked away.

"It is hard, very hard indeed, for wealthy people to enter God's kingdom," he said. "It is easier for a camel to get through the eye of a needle!"

One day some mothers brought their children to Jesus.

"We'd like him to say a blessing for them," they explained to the disciples.

"No!" said the disciples. "Jesus has all kinds of people who need to talk to him. Important people, as it happens."

Jesus heard what they said. He came over straight away.

"Let the children come to me," he said. "Do not try to stop them.

"The kingdom of heaven belongs to such as these."

FRIENDS AND ENEMIES

Wherever Jesus went, crowds flocked to see him. Many were enthusiastic about his teaching.

Not so the Pharisees and the rabbis. They were deeply suspicious. One day they came from far and wide to listen to his teaching, to try to spot the faults.

On that day some men arrived at the house where Jesus was. They were carrying a friend who could not walk. They were hoping that Jesus would heal him.

"But how do we get to Jesus?" they puzzled. "The house is full already. We can't just push our way through."

Then, in a moment of inspiration, they hurried up the outside steps to the flat roof.

They scrabbled through the tiles to make a hole.

They tied ropes to each corner of their friend's sleeping mat. Then they lowered their friend down right in front of Jesus.

Jesus smiled.

"My friend, your sins are forgiven," he said.

The rabbis and the Pharisees began murmuring to each other.

"Did you hear that? It's exactly as we feared.

"What he said is blasphemy: Jesus is claiming to be God! Only God can forgive sins!"

Jesus looked at them steadily.

"Anyone can say the words, 'Your sins are forgiven,' he explained. But does the person who says them have the authority? Are the sins forgiven?

"I will show you that I do speak with authority. I'm going to say something much more difficult."

He spoke to the man.

"Get up off your mat and walk!" he declared.

At once the man got up, rolled up his sleeping mat, and looked around in astonishment.

"Well, what can I say?" the man said nervously. "I know: Praise the Lord! Praise the Lord."

He went on his way, leaving the rabbis and Pharisees totally dumbfounded.

Jesus and the Sabbath

One sabbath day, Jesus and his disciples were walking through some harvest fields. His disciples picked some ears of corn, rubbed them in their hands, and began to eat the grain.

Some Pharisees saw them. "How dare you do that! The Commandments forbid any work on the sabbath."

Jesus turned to face them. "Haven't you read about what David did when his men were hungry? He went into the place of worship and took the bread that had been offered to God.

"The sabbath exists to serve people, not condemn them."

On another sabbath, Jesus was teaching in a synagogue. A man there had a paralysed hand.

Some Pharisees were also there, once again eager to criticize Jesus for any fault.

Jesus called the man to the front. "Put your hand out," he asked.

The man did so. At once he could move it as well as his good hand.

The Pharisees were angry and gleeful at the same time.

"Another crime against the sabbath," they agreed. "We'll find a way to punish Jesus."

JESUS AND THE STORM

Jesus and his disciples often went by boat. It was the simplest way to reach the many towns and villages on the shore of Lake Galilee.

At the end of one particular day, Jesus asked his disciples to sail the boat to the other side of the lake.

Jesus was tired after a day's preaching. He fell asleep.

Suddenly a strong wind blew up. The wind howled. The waves rocked the boat.

The fishermen among the group had sailed many storms. This time, however, they were terrified.

"Wake Jesus up! We need everyone to help bail the water from the boat.

"Hurry up, or we'll all drown!"

Jesus got up. "Be still," he commanded the wind. "Lie down," he told the waves.

At once the lake was calm.

Jesus looked sternly at his disciples. "Have you no faith?" he asked.

They looked at each other in amazement and concern.

"Jesus can be scarier than any storm," whispered one.

"Who can he be, that even the wind and waves obey him?"

JAIRUS AND HIS DAUGHTER

From the shore, people could see the boat arriving. "Jesus is coming," they exclaimed excitedly. "Get ready to cheer!" Among them was a man named Jairus.

He was more impatient than anyone to see Jesus... but not to cheer.

As Jesus stepped ashore, Jairus flung himself at his feet.

"Please help me. My young daughter is dreadfully ill. Please heal her before she dies."

Jesus agreed to come and help, but it was slow going. So many people seemed to want to speak to Jesus.

At once point, Jesus even stopped.

"Someone touched me," he said. "Someone who needed my help touched me."

A woman nodded and bit her lip. "I'm sorry," she said. "It was me. And I know I've been healed. I felt better at once."

Jesus smiled. "Your faith has made you well," he said.

He set off again with Jairus. Then a messenger from Jairus' house came hurrying up.

"There's no need to trouble the Teacher now," he said. "I'm so sorry. Your little girl... she's died."

Jairus began to shake with grief.

"Don't be afraid," said Jesus. "Only believe, and she will be well."

He went to the house.

Mourners had already gathered outside to weep and wail. Jesus sent them away.

He went into the house, and to the room where the girl lay, pale and still.

Jesus took her hand: "Little girl, get up," he said.

She sat up at once.

Jairus and his wife could hardly believe their eyes. Grief turned to astonishment, wonder, and joy.

Jesus spoke to them softly.

"She'll be hungry," he said. "I think it's time to get her something to eat."

WHO IS JESUS?

One day, Jesus had gone off by himself to pray. His disciples came looking for him.

He asked them a question:

"Who do the crowds say I am?"

"Some think you're John the Baptist," they replied. "We all know he ran in to trouble with the ruler of Galilee and was executed. But people think you're John brought back to life.

"Others think you're Elijah," they said. "Still others think you're one of the other great prophets of days gone by."

"And you?" asked Jesus. "Who do you say I am?

Peter replied at once:

"You're God's messiah," he said.

Jesus nodded solemnly. "You are not to tell anyone about this conversation.

"Just remember this. I am going to be rejected by the rabbis and the priests and all the people who count themselves as leaders of the Jewish faith.

"I will be put to death, but three days later I will rise again.

"If any of you want to come with me, you are going to have to forget your own plans, take up your cross, and follow me.

"You will have your reward in God's kingdom."

The good Samaritan

The religious leaders grew ever more eager to trap Jesus.

One day a teacher of the Law came to him with a question. He hoped to trick him.

"What must I do to receive eternal life?" he asked.

Jesus' reply was simple: "What do the Scriptures say?"

"Now the answer to that is easy," replied the teacher. " 'Love the Lord your God with all your heart, with all your soul, with all your strength, and with all your mind'; and then 'Love your neighbour as you love yourself'."

"Quite right," said Jesus. "You have the answer."

The teacher did not want to be brushed aside like that.

"Who is my neighbour?" he protested.

Jesus told a story.

"There was once a man who was going from Jerusalem to Jericho. The road passes through wild, open country. There, robbers ambushed him. They beat him up, took all he had, and left him for dead in the road.

"It so happened that a priest from the Temple was on the road that day. He saw the body in the road but did not want anything to do with it. He hurried by on the other side.

"Another official from the Temple came by. He sidled close to take a look at the body. Then he too hurried on his way.

"A Samaritan came by."

The teacher of the Law cringed a little at this. Samaritans were the foreigners who had been settled in Israel in the time of the Assyrians.

"The Samaritan saw the body in the road. He felt sorry for the man. At once he went over and bandaged the man's wounds. Then he lifted him on to his donkey and took him to an inn.

"He stayed that night to take care of the stranger he had helped. In the morning he had to travel on. Before he left, he gave money to the innkeeper. 'So you can look after the man at my expense,' he explained."

Jesus looked at the teacher.

"Now tell me: which of the three passers-by was neighbour to the man?"

"The one who was kind to him," came the reply.

"Then you go and act in the same way as he did," said Jesus.

JESUS AND THE MAN BORN BLIND

One day Jesus was walking along a road when they saw a man who had been born blind.

"Why is he blind?" the disciples asked. "Is he guilty of some wrongdoing, or is it the fault of his parents?"

"Neither," replied Jesus. "He is blind so we can see God's power at work in him. While I am in the world, I am light for the world."

Jesus spat on the ground and mixed it with the dirt to make mud. He put this on the man's eyes and then told him to go and wash it off.

When the man did so, he could see.

The Pharisees heard news of the miracle. They summoned the man and asked him to tell them what had happened.

When he told his story, they shook their heads.

"The man who did this can't be from God," they told him. "He breaks the law of the sabbath."

Other people disagreed. "How can he cure blindness unless he came from God?" they asked the Pharisees.

Once again the Pharisees asked to talk to the man who had been healed.

"We simply don't believe your story," they said. "That Jesus is a dreadful sinner. "

"I don't know about that," replied the man. "All I know is this: once I was blind; now I can see."

That made the Pharisees very angry. "You're a sinner as well," they cried. "From now on you are forbidden to enter our synagogue."

When Jesus heard, he went to find the man, who explained what had happened.

"I still believe in you," he declared.

Jesus smiled slightly and then he sighed. "It's the Pharisees who are blind," he said. "They refuse to see the truth about me.

"I am the good shepherd. I am willing to die for my flock of followers. The Father loves me because I am willing to give up my life, in order that I may receive it back again."

People who heard what he said did not know what to make of his words.

"Is he mad? Is he possessed by some evil force?"

"No," others replied. "A man possessed would not say such things. How could someone with an evil spirit give sight to the blind?

The disagreement could not be resolved.

Many people loved and respected Jesus.

Others were determined to get rid of him.

An End and a Beginning

One day, Jesus called his disciples aside. He wanted to speak to them in private.

"We are going to Jerusalem," he said. "Everything the prophets said about the Son of Man is going to come true. The rabbis and the chief priests will have him put to death. Three days later he will rise again."

The disciples looked puzzled. Jesus often said puzzling things.

ZACCHAEUS

The road to Jerusalem that Jesus chose went through Jericho.

There was a tax collector there named Zacchaeus.

Everyone in Jericho hated him: he overcharged people when he collected the tax money. He had made himself wealthy at their expense.

Zacchaeus was as eager as anyone to see Jesus, but there was a problem. He was very short. The crowds who so disliked him would not let him through to the front.

Then he had an idea: he could climb a tree!

He had a perfect view of Jesus as he and his disciples came near.

To Zacchaeus' astonishment, Jesus stopped. He looked up.

"Come down, Zacchaeus," he called. "I want to come to your house today."

Zacchaeus was astonished.

So were the townspeople. They grumbled noisily as Zacchaeus came slithering down the tree and then led Jesus to his grand house.

"Would you believe it?" they muttered. "The great teacher has gone to have a meal at the home of a sinner.

"How very wrong!"

Whatever it was that Jesus said to Zacchaeus that day made a real difference.

At the end of the meal, the tax collector stood up to make an announcement.

"From today I'm going to change my ways," he said. "I'm going to give half of what I own to the poor. If I ever cheated anyone, I will pay them back four times what I took."

Jesus smiled. "Today this man has acted like a true descendant of Abraham. The Son of Man came to seek and save the lost."

TO JERUSALEM

It was nearly Passover time. Many people were on the way to Jerusalem. They all wanted to celebrate the festival at the Temple there.

As they came near to the city, Jesus sent his disciples to fetch a donkey. He wanted to ride into Jerusalem.

The crowds made way for the donkey. They saw who was riding it. They began to whisper.

"It's Jesus! Perhaps he is going to declare himself our king."

Suddenly someone shouted, "God bless the king! God bless the king."

Almost at once, more people joined in... and then more.

Soon the ride to Jerusalem had become a parade. People broke off palm branches to wave in celebration. Others laid their cloaks on the ground for the donkey to walk on.

Some Pharisees in the crowd marched angrily towards Jesus. "Teacher, you must tell your followers to be quiet."

Jesus shook his head. "Even if I did, the stones would begin to shout. No one could hide the meaning of what is happening."

Jesus reached the city and went to the Temple.

The courtyard was full of people.

Traders had set up their stalls, selling the items that people needed for the festival.

They were changing money for the Temple coins.

They had sheep and doves to offer as sacrifices.

Jesus frowned. Then he cried aloud. "This place is meant to be a house of prayer," he said. "You have made it into a den of thieves."

He tipped up one trader's table, and then another… and another.

Coins jingled to the ground. The animals for sale began to run. The dove cages tumbled over and the doves flew free.

The chief priests were furious. They began to whisper among themselves.

"This must be the time to get rid of him," they agreed. "But how can we arrest him? The crowds hang on his every word."

In the next few days, Jesus often came back to the Temple with his disciples. There he preached to anyone who would listen.

It was at this time that one of Jesus' own disciples turned against his master.

Judas Iscariot decided to side with the chief priests.

He went to talk to them about how he could help them catch Jesus when he was alone.

They were delighted, and offered to pay.

Judas accepted the money. He began looking for the opportunity he needed.

THE LAST SUPPER

The day came for the Jewish people to celebrate the Passover meal. Once again they would remember the story of the escape from slavery in Egypt. Once again they would remember the giving of the Law to Moses. Once again they would remember their covenant with God: if they would obey the Law, then God would be their God, and they would be God's people.

Jesus sent Peter and John to prepare the room he had agreed to borrow. As evening came, he and the twelve disciples gathered at the table.

In the midst of the usual traditions, Jesus took a piece of bread, gave thanks to God, broke it, and gave it to them, saying, "This is my body, which is given for you. Do this in memory of me."

In the same way he gave them a cup of wine after the supper, saying, "This cup is God's new covenant sealed with my blood, which is poured out for you."

Then he paused and looked around at each of them.

"The person who will betray me is here at this table. The Son of Man will die as God has decided, but it will be terrible for the one who betrays him."

Peter was eager to reply.

"I'm ready to go to prison with you. I'll die with you if I have to!"

Jesus shook his head. "Before the cock crows to mark tomorrow's dawn, you will deny that you know me. You will do so three times."

Jesus went on to remind all of his disciples how they should live.

"The greatest among you must be like the youngest," he said. "The leader must be like the servant."

He gave them a new commandment:

"Love one another."

At some point in the evening – no one quite noticed at the time – Judas Iscariot slipped away.

Betrayed

Night was falling as Jesus and his eleven faithful disciples left Jerusalem. They went to an olive grove nearby: the Garden of Gethsemane. There they planned to sleep out under the stars.

Jesus took himself apart from his friends and began to pray.

"Father God," he wept, "if it is possible, may I escape the suffering that is to come.

"Not my will, however, but your will be done."

When he went back to his disciples he found them all asleep.

"Wake up!" he said. "Pray that you will not face the trial that is to come!"

As he was speaking, Judas came back. He kissed Jesus in greeting.

"Is that how you betray me?" said Jesus sadly.

For behind Judas came Jesus' accusers: the chief priests and other leaders of the people, along with officers of the Temple guard.

They arrested Jesus and took him to the house of the High Priest.

Peter followed at a distance. When he reached the house, he stayed outside in the

courtyard, half hiding in the shadows.

A servant woman saw him. "I've seen you before!" she said. "You were with Jesus."

"I don't even know him," Peter growled in reply.

Later a manservant saw Peter.

"You're one of those disciples, too!" he declared.

"No, I'm not!" retorted Peter.

About an hour later another man came up and pointed a finger at him. "There's no doubt this man is one of Jesus' friends. Listen to his accent: he's from Galilee."

Peter clenched his fists as he answered, "I don't know what you're talking about."

As he did so, a cockerel crowed the dawn.

Peter remembered what Jesus had said.

He had denied his friend, his teacher, his master.

He left the courtyard, found a quiet place, and broke down in tears.

CONDEMNED

Jesus was put on trial. He faced a council of the priests and the leading rabbis.

"So tell us: are you the messiah?" they asked.

Jesus answered, "If I tell you, you will not believe me; and if I ask you a question, you will not answer. But from now on the Son of Man will be seated on the right of Almighty God."

"Are you the Son of God?" they asked.

"You say that I am," replied Jesus.

His words were greeted with a clamour of protest.

"That's all we need to hear!" they declared. "It remains only for the Roman governor to pass the sentence."

In the morning Jesus was taken to face the governor, Pontius Pilate.

The priests set out the charge. "This man claims to be our messiah.

"That means he wants to be our king. That is in defiance of Roman rule. For that, he deserves to die."

The Roman knew little of the Jewish concerns. The preacher from Galilee didn't look like a rebel. He hadn't done anything to threaten Roman rule.

"I can't see any reason to condemn him," he declared. "I am willing to have him whipped and then let him go. It's the custom to free one of your prisoners at festival time."

Indeed, a crowd had gathered outside the governor's residence to make sure that the custom was followed.

"Set Barabbas free! Set Barabbas free!" they began to chant.

They were making their appeal for a man accused of riot and murder.

"This year I'm choosing to set Jesus free," announced Pilate.

The crowd responded with fury.

"Crucify him! Crucify him!" they shouted.

Pilate sensed their anger. He began to fear a riot.

He ordered Barabbas to be set free. He passed the sentence of death on Jesus.

Roman soldiers took Jesus away.

They read the notice of his crime that Pilate has written:

"Jesus of Nazareth, King of the Jews."

"A king, are you?" they mocked. "Here, let's dress you up in this purple robe.

"And we have a crown: just like the emperor's crown. Except that his is made of laurel, and yours is from thorns."

For a while they bullied and abused their prisoner.

Then they forced him to carry a heavy cross of wood to the place of execution: a hill named Golgotha, just outside the city walls.

There they crucified him: nailing him to the cross by his hands and feet.

They nailed the notice of his crime above him and hoisted the cross upright.

"Forgive them, father," prayed Jesus. "They don't know what they are doing."

Two other men were crucified that day – men who had been condemned as criminals.

For many hours, under dark and sunless sky, they hung in agony.

Then Jesus cried out in a loud voice: "Father, into your hands I place my spirit."

With these words, he died.

Somewhere, not far off, Judas Iscariot wept for his guilt and shame. He took his own life, alone and despised.

A NEW BEGINNING

On the afternoon that Jesus died, a man named Joseph, who was from Arimathea, went to Pilate.

"Please allow me to take Jesus' body," he said. "I will arrange for it to be buried."

He had the body wrapped in linen and laid in a rock-cut tomb.

Some women who had been followers of Jesus watched as the stone door was rolled in place.

But already the sun was setting. Soon it would be the sabbath day of rest. Jesus' followers spent the day in deepest sorrow.

Early on the Sunday morning, some women went back to the tomb.

To their astonishment and dismay, the stone door had been rolled aside. The tomb was empty.

As they stood there wondering, two people in bright shining clothes came and stood beside them. "Why are you looking among the dead for one who is alive?" they asked. "He is not here. He has been raised to life."

After that, Jesus' friends and followers began to see the one they thought was dead for ever.

There in the garden, Mary from Magdala saw a man she thought was the gardener. When the man turned and said her name, she knew it was Jesus.

Later, in Galilee, Peter and some of the other disciples went fishing. As they sailed back to shore in the dawn light, they saw someone cooking breakfast on a charcoal fire. It was Jesus.

Peter was ashamed of having fled from danger on the night of the arrest. Jesus asked him to take care of his flock of followers.

The day came when Jesus appeared to all his disciples together.

"Everything has happened as the Scriptures foretold," he said to them. "Now I am sending you to preach the message I gave you: the message of repentance, and the forgiveness of sins.

"But wait a while: God will send his Holy Spirit to give you the strength you need to do so."

With these words, Jesus was taken up into heaven.

Some ten days later, on the day of the festival of Pentecost, Jesus' followers were in a room in Jerusalem together.

They were still afraid that the Jewish leaders were determined to find them and punish them.

Suddenly they heard a noise like a rushing wind. They saw flames of fire dancing above their heads.

They were filled with God's Holy Spirit.

At once they went out and began to preach the news about Jesus.

Many believed their preaching. They baptized those who wanted to be followers of Jesus: in the name of God the Father, God the Son, and God the Holy Spirit.

BIBLE REFERENCES